*What's the point of the church being a glo..... ......, ., ...
another? Or worse, if only some members of the family get to do all the
talking? It is vital that the voices of the global church are heard by those in the
western churches who have tended to listen only to themselves – especially
when those voices are speaking from the cutting edge of the church's mission.
So I heartily commend the vision and intentions of this project.*

Christopher J. H. Wright, Langham Partnership

*Mission is about encounters and participating in what God is doing to bring
about God's kingdom. The new Global Voices Series is a wonderful project that
gives voice to those who have been engaged in God's mission for many
decades, but whose voices have not yet been heard in much of the world.
Through these books, God's people will be challenged and encouraged to think
about and to practice mission in transformative ways; we will hear God's call
anew in the unique contexts these texts reflect and we will learn how to
participate again in our service to the kingdom of Christ.*

Rosalee Velloso Ewell, PhD, Principal, Redcliffe College
Executive Director, Theological Commission, World Evangelical Alliance

*The books in this collection expose us to connected themes which provide a
foundational canvas for Christianity throughout the world. They approach
mission as a challenging invitation to be born again, to break paradigms, to
rupture with and change the cultural perspectives with which one perceives the
world – our "Worldviews". They also highlight the need for a profound
transformation of our understanding of the Great Commission, suggesting that
this is more than just a cross-cultural task, but that it also includes labouring to
manifest the Kingdom of God in our daily life space, within our families and
our workplaces. Finally, the books in this series also present a valuable
approach that broadens the concept of mission itself: salvation through rebirth
cannot be merely understood anthropocentrically. Its blessing must reach* all of
creation. *It becomes clear that to fulfil the cultural mandate of Gen. 2:15 it is
also necessary to know and understand the functioning of creation as an
ecosystem.*

Marina da Silva, Former Brazilian Senator,
Minister of Environment and 2018 Presidential candidate

I have often lamented the fact that much of the most ground-breaking contextual theology is being done in languages that are largely inaccessible to the majority of the world's theologians. I have also often encouraged younger theologians that, instead of learning the classic languages of French and German, they should learn Spanish, or Korean, or Tagalog, or Indonesian. While learning these languages – or some of them – is still necessary today, Regnum Books is providing a great service to the future of theology by inaugurating this series in which hitherto inaccessible, major theological and missiological works will be translated into English. This is one of the most exciting projects that I have ever heard about, and one that has the potential to change the face of theology in our time. Now we are much closer to listening to all the voices!

Stephen Bevans, SVD
Louis J. Luzbetak, SVD Professor of Mission and Culture, Emeritus
Catholic Theological Union, Chicago, USA

English readers will benefit from the wisdom of majority world theologians writing for their own contexts – what a rare and significant contribution to enrich the church.

Dr Kang San Tan, General Director of BMS World Mission

All Are Called

Ao amado irmão em Cristo
Rafael, chamado para ser
sal e luz neste mundo em
trevas.

Mt 28:18-20

London, 20/3/2022

Pr Carvalho

Series Preface

The **Global Voices** series takes the missiological work of writers who have written in their own language and makes this accessible to the English-speaking world through translation and republishing. The key principle here is that the translated work reflects the context, experience and thinking of the local context. In so doing, Regnum Books seeks to amplify voices less easily heard outside their own contexts. Work of this nature will make a significant contribution to the development of 'polycentric missiology'; namely, mission thinking and practice that truly reflects the contexts, concerns and contributions of the global church in all its rich diversity.

Series Editors

Paul Bendor-Samuel	Executive Director, Oxford Centre for Mission Studies
Mark Greenwood	BMS Regional Leader for South America and Sub-Saharan Africa
Timóteo Carriker	Mission educator and consultant to the Brazilian Bible Society

REGNUM GLOBAL VOICES

All Are Called
Mission Strategies for Home

Rubem Amorese

Translated by Joyce Every-Clayton

Regnum is an imprint of the Oxford Centre for Mission Studies
St. Philip and St. James Church
Woodstock Road
Oxford OX2 6HR, UK
www.ocms.ac.uk/regnum

09 08 07 06 05 04 03 7 6 5 4 3 2 1

British Library Cataloguing in Publication Data
A catalogue record for this book is available from the British Library

ISBN: 978-1-912343-96-6

Typeset by Words by Design
Printed and bound by CPI Group (UK) Ltd,
Croydon, CR0 4YY

The publication of this volume is made possible through the
financial assistance of **Evangelisches Missionswerk** and the
Baptist Missionary Society.

Contents

Preface

Layperson and *missionary* – two words the devil loves to use in the church simply because they set limits that are perfectly suited to his way of working. The first disqualifies the vast majority of Christians by putting them in the category of mere helpers in the church's missionary task, while the second qualifies a small minority as the only ones who have the responsibility of accomplishing this task. By means of these two words, the devil has managed to deliver a knockout blow to the majority of Christians.

It is strange to note that the word 'mission' appears only twice in the New Testament.[1] The first occurrence is in Acts 12:25 and refers to the return of Paul and Barnabas to Jerusalem, having been sent out from there on a missionary journey. The second is in 1 Timothy 2:15 and refers to motherhood and the mission of giving birth to the children God entrusts to mothers as part of their participation in creation. These two distinct occurrences of 'mission' in the New Testament help us to understand that 'mission' is not only what Paul and Barnabas did on their journey but is also what mothers do when they give birth and raise children. This is what this book is all about.

All Are Called is an attempt to banish the word *layperson* from our vocabulary and to present a more comprehensive and biblical understanding of the word *missionary*. The apostle Paul, as he travelled round preaching, was no more missionary than a mother who gives birth to children and dedicates herself (alongside the father, of course) to their upbringing. This helps us to see that Christ's call to follow him is a call to mission that involves *all* Christians in *all* that they do, regardless of whether they are called to go to a distant place to plant a church, or to be a civil servant, or to work at the important task of parenting. The truth Rubem Amorese addresses here is both simple and challenging: if we were as consecrated and as responsible in the way we act in our own localities, communities, professions or families as those missionaries who go out from our midst to other countries or ethnic groups, we would have a strong and committed 'Jerusalem' and our local churches and families would become a 'missionary factory'.

Missionaries who go to other countries have a strong conviction of calling; those who stay at home have no conviction of calling. The former prepare for their tasks and consecrate their lives to their mission; the latter just get on with life, with no concern for preparation or consecration. The former are always taken up with their mission work as well as with reporting back to churches and involving them in the vision; the latter only do something 'missionary' at weekends, for they don't understand that their workplace and their homes are mission fields – after all, they are 'only lay people'.

That is why the devil likes the words *layperson* and *missionary*; they exclude most Christians from mission. Mothers and fathers do not recognise motherhood and fatherhood as mission and, in fact, in today's world many look on children as an inconvenience. Some choose not to have them, and those who have children delegate the mission of bringing them up to a school or even to a therapist (when not even the school can control their offspring) because, for many parents, the 'mission' of making money or striving for professional success is much more important. Such professionals don't recognise that the exercise of their professions in their many workplaces is God's means of fulfilling his mission in the world. Students spend much of their lives in schools and universities without recognising the need to prepare for a rich and vast mission field. We think in this way because, after all, we're just lay people, not missionaries; we're in 'Jerusalem', not in Myanmar.

However, mission always begins in 'Jerusalem', at home, in the local community. It's not a question of missionary projects that involve a few, but of a missionary consciousness to which God calls all Christians. Abraham Kuyper was a Dutch Christian who lived at the turn of the 20th century; he was a pastor, journalist, politician and teacher. As a journalist, he began a newspaper and wrote numerous articles. As Prime Minister, he founded the Free University of Amsterdam and revolutionised the educational system of the Netherlands. In all these areas, whether as a politician or pastor of a local church, he retained the same conscious awareness of vocation. He said that every morning, on waking, he would look at a cross at the head of his bed and, as it were, hear God telling him that everything in his life belonged to him. He consecrated his life to God and dedicated it to the task of making 'Jerusalem' his mission field.

You will come face to face with a new missionary challenge in this book as you realise that *you* are a missionary; you, and not just the others sent to some distant country; and your mission field is all those places where you have opportunities to accomplish something for the Kingdom of God. As we all begin to think and act in this way, our families and churches will be transformed into 'missionary factories' whose activities will shine in every corner of the earth and make the glory of God visible to all.

Ricardo Barbosa

Introduction

When I was a boy in Rio de Janeiro, my school sponsored an outing to the Kibon[2] ice cream factory– and what a delight it was! In addition to receiving detailed information about the ice cream manufacturing process – hygiene, automation, product shelf-life and the decision-making process concerning flavours, we were allowed to try out as many flavours as we wanted during the visit. Today I understand and value this public relations strategy, now adopted by factories and institutions round the world. That's why I'm still talking about it fifty years later, and even today, my personal celebrations must include some good old Kibon ice cream.

This idea of the factory visit in order to get to know the product in detail – all accompanied by the affective side-effects – resurfaces here in my reflections on the ministry of reconciliation. By the way, those last words constitute the overarching frame of my reflection: our 'mission' makes us not just *missionaries* but *ministers*.

Don't miss the emotional component of the book evident in my short phrase 'the affective side-effects'. Of course, that is one of the objectives of the 'factory visit' and good PR strategy. In a similar fashion, there is no way we can approach the subject dealt with in this book by cold light of reason alone; we are talking about our lives here. It's a bit like football. Everybody knows something about it and everybody can recall good and bad experiences. And it is the affective element that causes these impressions to last throughout the believer's life, and which either motivates him to work on the subject or turns him away from it.

I like to think of myself as being someone who has life pretty well sorted out, with my mind made up about most things. Perhaps that's to do with age – which compels us to accept syntheses. However, when it comes to missions, I am anything but sorted out; rather, I am a Christian plagued by ambiguities and unanswered questions. Not forgetting the sympathies, antipathies, and (I have to confess) disagreements with no plausible justification. Probably they have an emotional origin, affective side-effects of past conflicts. Nevertheless, I have decided to revisit these ghosts of my personal story in search of one more existential synthesis. And I'm doing this by way of a 'visit to the missionary factory'. The account which follows is the story of my visit. What's more, I invite you to accompany me as I describe my journey in search of some personal coherence on the subject.

Don't be alarmed if you don't find me to be a wise master who will guide you along safe paths, for that is not what I will be doing. The truth is that I don't intend to hide the problems that arise from my own doubts and ambiguities; so look on the reflections that follow more as *confessions*. And, should you perchance 'find yourself' in some of them, maybe you will feel like walking a mile or two along the road and be blessed as you do.

The confessional nature of this text makes it more a set of short sermons than well-elaborated lessons, more synthetic reflection than analytical explanation. My purpose and overriding hope is to inspire reflection, self-analysis and personal conclusions.

I try to give consistency to the confessional proposal by making the text gravitate round some images – or perhaps I should call them parables. The first, in addition to the visit to the missionary factory itself, is *The Parable of the Onion,* which describes a way of getting to the heart of an issue by removing layer after layer – something which can bring tears to one's eyes. The second, *The Parable of the Worship Service round the Campfire*, describes some moments of emotional appeals and calls for consecration which I found difficult, causing inner conflicts. The third is *The Parable of the Veterinary Surgeon*, my image of the incarnation: that special doctor of my childhood dreams, who was able to understand and heal animals' pains without their needing to explain anything to him. Animals don't talk. The fourth and last is *The Parable of the Priestly Order of Foot-Washing*, my way of describing a special, solemn missionary commissioning, accompanied by anointing and consecration.

The book that follows turns on these four images, and it is my sincere prayer that my reflections-cum-confessions may help us all to sort out some of our own personal questions, as far as the missionary mandate of every one of Christ's disciples is concerned.

Rubem Amorese

1. Who's Afraid of the Missionary?

From time to time, Claudia Kern, our missionary in Asia, returns to Brasilia to spend time with her family, and she is always invited to share her experiences with the church. There are lots of stories, slides, photographs, prayers and offerings. Her reports and testimonies leave us all humbled, even if that is not her intention. My feeling is that it is a time when we in the church face uncomfortable contradictions.

It's always the same when a missionary comes to visit. On the one hand, the church is happy to play its part in the challenge, to invest in missions. On the other hand, we feel humbled by these glorious missionary testimonies which almost suggest that everyone should be living life with the same courage, zeal, boldness in prayer and evangelism, dependent on the Lord in everything, and totally available to others.

And I wonder if God might be using these visitors to exhort us to a life of greater devotion? Maybe we don't understand that we too are missionaries. Maybe we're unaware that we too have been given this inescapable ministry of reconciliation, either because – to our shame – we do not exercise it, or because we do not see it as a distinctive in the life of the church.

It seems to me that if those of us who remain at home are also missionaries, we lack something of what Claudia has, something that could clarify and define our position even without having to move to the other side of the world. If we are not doing our part but living lethargic, comfortable lives, we need to listen to our conscience. Otherwise, why do we feel uncomfortable? Could it be a false accusation from the enemy?

These thoughts have led me to consider my own history in relation to the missionary call. I will write more about it later on, but for now, I share the thought that many of us did not experience the inevitable call to mission which was supposed to accompany the famous time around the campfire: we simply did not have a specific call to *intro-mission*, mission to those we meet every day. As a result, we have not been formally sent out to our mission posts, to our homes, neighbourhoods, schools or workplaces. In fact, few churches develop strategies in support of this type of mission. Few lay hands on a young couple thinking about marriage; and later on, when they present their child to God before the church, they are not told that they are being sent on a mission of the utmost importance. Infant baptism, in the churches where it is practised, does include an element of commitment on the part of the parents, and in many cases the ceremony is *almost* a commissioning service.[3] However, as far as I have observed, there is no explicit mention of the parents' *mission* to their children. Maybe just for the simple reason that the concept of being invested with the specific mission of *'going' to their child and making him or her a disciple* is missing.

It may be, reader, that your experience is different, that your church does these things consciously and as a matter of routine. Thank God for that! But where I've been, I notice an absence of the most important missionary vision of all, one that gets right to the heart of the issue. One important result, to give a strategic example which we will look at later, is that it is not clear to many of our young people that a marriage to someone without the same life mission, whether that be with a non-Christian (a mixed marriage) or with a Christian who has other projects, could jeopardise all their missionary plans.

To be fair, a spouse may not feel under any obligation to accompany the other in his or her mission, because the subject had not been discussed or even regarded as fundamental during the period of courtship. In so many areas, their interests and desires will be very different: questions related to prayer and vigils, ways of dealing with frustration, the preaching of the Word, a simple lifestyle, Kingdom values, bringing up children, options for leisure, the use of family time and so on. Depending on their relationship with God, one spouse may not even be able to accompany the other in their activities, for these are priorities of a Kingdom to which he or she may not even belong. Unless led by the Spirit, most certainly the other will not share such a call. This leads me to observe that many of our discussions about whether or not such a marriage is an 'unequal yoke' and about what that means, are very superficial.

Often the scenario becomes even more confusing when the unbelieving spouse seems to be a better person than the believer. It is not uncommon – and pure sectarianism – for Christians to decide that the believing partner must be the good element in an 'unequally yoked' marriage as far as issues of life mission are concerned, and that the unbeliever is always a dead weight to be dragged along. And all because the church either passed no clear, strategic message to the young people about their missionary call, or because their call was not taken sufficiently seriously when the young person was choosing a spouse.

Of course, one should not rule out the possibility of our making wrong choices even when the path ahead is clear. We all make mistakes and not always out of ignorance. So it's good to recognise that it is difficult for a young man to choose the Cross instead of following his own heart. But it is also good to conclude these thoughts by remembering that the call is for everyone: *If any man will come after me, let him deny himself, take up his cross and follow me* (Mark 8:34).

So we begin to realise that these decisions that can seem so insignificant demand tremendous power. Power to draw our own 'red lines' on the ground of our lives and not go beyond the limits set; power to tame our own wills; power to put the Lord on the throne of our heart, that heart which we know to be deceitful. Power to say 'No!' to life's short cuts.

We often ask God for power for our missionaries. As we imagine the difficulties they face in a strange country with a different culture and language, we plead with God with great urgency, asking him to pour out his power on them. But we usually forget to ask ourselves the question: Why not plead for the same power on *our* lives? For example, as we consider our missionary vision, do we need less of God's power as we choose a spouse? Less of God's power as we set aside good looks and prefer companionship and a unity of purpose? Less of God's power as we wait for years while that special someone does not turn up – and risk living the rest of our life in celibacy?

How much power does it take to be a good father, a good husband or a good son, and by this example witness to the salvation found in Christ? Less than that needed by a cross-cultural missionary? How much power does it take to serve my brothers and sisters joyfully in the everyday things of life, to be simply helpful to them instead of being of no use to them? How much power does it take to put the newspaper aside and give attention to my child? To discipline him or her in a biblical manner, with serenity, meekness and firmness – and all after a hard day at work? To administer discipline in such a way that the child understands that I am doing it out of real love? How much power do I need to be genuinely interested in my work colleague, to the point of longing for his salvation? To the point of praying for him daily, and pleading for God to give me opportunities to serve and witness in such a way that he comes to understand the gospel?

Yes, I am talking about power to *be*. Actually, I would prefer to use the word 'grace', but because I do not want anyone to be in doubt as to the origin of this amazing grace, I am speaking of the *power* promised in Acts 1:8: *But you will receive power when the Holy Spirit comes on you; and you will be my witnesses.* Power to witness by our lives that, in the Gospel, there is salvation for everyone who believes; that redemption and a transformed life are possible, whether the person is a Jew or a Greek, within the church or an outsider. There is no distinction (Romans 1:15-16).

Let me develop these thoughts. Why do we think that this divine power is distributed in small amounts – drop by drop, as it were – and that only missionaries in faraway places have a right to it? Why is it that theirs are the only tasks that need a special divine anointing? Is it just a question of distance – the farther from home you are, the more of God you need? Could that be why we speak of 'missions' in the plural as a synonym of distance, and only rarely use the singular, 'mission', with its connotations of a task to be fulfilled, a call, a role, a ministry?

Well, I decided to think more about this and to 'peel the onion' of the missionary mandate. The metaphor I have chosen to deal with issues that are central to the argument of this book comes from the frequently tearful process of taking an onion apart layer by layer right down to the core. To peel the missionary onion is to ask: How are missionaries born? Where do they come from? Where are they going? What are they doing? Why are they doing what they do?

Hopefully, this reflection will help us understand better the reason why we no longer send our own sons and daughters to distant places. We send only other people's offspring and, although we have no idea of their upbringing, we exhort them to teach *the whole counsel of God* in some faraway country.

The problem is that, for this to happen, we have to trust that their academic education will fill the gaps in the training they did not receive at home, that powerful training that comes from our own lived example. We expect that those who teach them missions will give them what we did not know how to give them when they were children. And we want to believe that, at the end of their missionary preparation course, they will know, as if by the magic power of Pentecost, how to build families or churches. Families of God (Ephesians 2:27), families like those we would like to have given them, but to which we did not commit our very soul in earnest prayer. Maybe because we didn't know that the subject was so important.

So this is our theme: 'Mission Jerusalem'. Why 'Jerusalem'? Let's look more closely at our key text: *But you will receive power when the Holy Spirit comes on you; and you will be my witnesses in Jerusalem, and in all Judea and Samaria, and to the ends of the earth* (Acts 1:8). There it is: Jerusalem was the first mission field Jesus designated for the church that would be formed at Pentecost; there the disciples were to wait for the promised Spirit. I hold that it is appropriate to conclude that 'Jerusalem' is the place where we already are, and that 'Judea' refers to our neighbours, followed by nearby towns, more distant cities, and of course indigenous peoples and faraway places.

A necessary confession: I am unable to speak about cross-cultural mission from personal, practical experience. My experience is purely academic, as is the case of many of those who teach candidates with a missionary call and prepare them for cross-cultural work. Such practical experience as I have is limited to the field of urban mission, and for this reason I leave the task of pronouncing authoritatively on cross-cultural mission to those who have actually done it. My intention is to look closely at 'Jerusalem' through missionary eyes, and to reflect on how what I see there might be incorporated into our knowledge and strategies for reaching Judea, Samaria and the ends of the earth.

The hope that motivates me is that a focus on 'Jerusalem' may contribute to our understanding of the whole missionary task. This book is not a criticism of 'missions'. Nor do I intend to make comparisons or choices between the near and the far. Much less do I criticise missionary research and the teaching of 'missions'. For an onion to have a centre it must have all the layers – my chief concern is with the centre, not with the specific layers.

The Missionary Factory

If Santa Claus's toy factory is located at the North Pole, the 'missionary factory' is located in 'Jerusalem'; if Santa Claus comes from the North Pole, missionaries come from 'Jerusalem', that town or city where you and I live. Having clarified that, we can now begin at the beginning.

It was Christmas, and I had fallen asleep while watching one of those Disney movies about Santa Claus, complete with North Pole, the obligatory elves and reindeer, and the traditional nibbles of walnuts, hazelnuts and baked ham with raisin stuffing. In these films, in addition to many other adventures, children visit Santa's toy factory. It reminded me of my visit to the ice cream factory as a boy, and the two experiences coalesced to give birth to the idea of visiting the 'missionary factory' to understand its most basic processes. Maybe even to discover if there are genuine reasons for the depression we feel on hearing the reports of our missionaries among Indian tribes or in far distant places.

So what is a missionary factory anyway? What are its basic processes? What does it produce? My replies to these questions will be somewhat autobiographical, and therefore partial. But it can still be described as a factory visit.

My earliest memories of the subject go back to my childhood. I was obliged to sit quietly through the missionary services and, alongside the adults, 'enjoy' complicated financial reports on missions. Especially during October, I would sell old newspapers and magazines as part of several fund-raising campaigns for the missionary work of the church. It was an act of faith, for I never saw this mysterious being they called a missionary. The picture I had in my mind was that of a saint, someone who never showed up because he was far above my ability to perceive him, a holy phantom player on the church team.

The Worship Time round the Campfire

As the years passed, the subject became more personal, because of the dreaded worship service round the campfire which was normally held on the last night of a Gospel camp. I simply didn't like that service, I cannot really say why. If I could, I would play truant. Many times I ended up going just to be with my friends, but I kept my distance, and if I needed to run and disappear into the darkness I didn't think twice about doing it.

It was all about emotional pressure. The problem was not just the appeals themselves, but also because I thought that the emotional element was overdone. There were always people crying everywhere. Worst of all was the moment when the preacher called us up to the front to volunteer to 'go'. This to the sound of quiet singing, with such words as: 'I will go, Lord / I will obey you / I want to speak, I want to pray / I will go, Lord.' That was my cue for disappearing into the darkness, even if I was risking being bitten by a snake.

Today I look back and realise how much I lost out by running away, for my resistance meant that many blessings passed me by. Many solemn promises, many decisions, many of the basic structures for life simply ricocheted off my armour and did not manage to reach into my heart. Because of my decisions to run from the camp, much of what my life walk could have been was lost; it was as if my cup had been turned upside-down and was therefore unable to catch the falling rain. Of course, I am speaking from a human perspective. God's take on these things is different. He knows.

What I can remember about my motives in those troubled days – and bearing in mind that teenage years have their own crises and characteristics – was that I had great reservations, both about the person who was doing the speaking and about the content of the appeal being made. I kept telling myself I would not fall for such patter. The fact is that, on most occasions, the speaker was a foreigner with a terrible accent or speaking through an interpreter, and as a result was a little distant, not to say suspect. It was hard for me to accept the authority and legitimacy of the appeal, because of my overly critical spirit. It was hard for me to consider the preacher as one of ours and, at the same time, admit the authority of his personal example. After all, he was, without a doubt, someone who had answered the call that he was reproducing at that moment in time. But he was a *gringo*. And when he wasn't a foreigner, he was just a team member. In my head, that meant 'indoctrinated', a one-track mind. It came to the same thing in the end for those who, like me, had emotional reservations – excessive reservations, I admit.

But there was also the detail of the objective content of those sermons. The appeals were always extreme. Complete surrender. Some even suggested that I would not return home afterwards 'if that is what God is asking'; that I should heed the call by faith; that I would leave the camp to go out to serve God.

However, I was afraid to hand my life over to people I did not know well. Or rather, to people I did not trust. (Today, I reckon I didn't trust God much either at that time). Not because the people themselves gave me any reason to distrust them, but because of stories I heard of how seminary students and missionary candidates suffered during their time of preparation. Gullible young people in the hand of tyrannical teachers who justified their behaviour on the grounds that the candidates were being prepared for worst-case scenarios. I came to have a very negative image of seminaries, Bible institutes and missionary training colleges. Of course, much of this aversion came from my own resistant heart.

As if that were not enough, the appeal made to the accompaniment of a crackling bonfire was for me to commit myself, by faith, to go wherever God would send me. And because the speaker was a *gringo* whose sermon illustrations came out of his own cross-cultural experience, I was sure that I would be sent to a distant country. Africa was always present in my nightmares about the subject. In those services, no-one ever spoke about urban mission. That mission field, the one nearest home, was only mentioned in appeals for conversion or consecration; only then were family, school, church and work referred to.

Thus, the prophet Isaiah would always send me overseas: *Then I heard the voice of the LORD saying, 'Whom shall I send? And who will go for us?' And I said, 'Here am I. Send me'* (Isaiah 6:8) – to Africa. But the appeal came up against a heart in crisis, suspicious. From one point of view, I now see that it was a heart that did not treat the things of God lightly. I wanted everything to be correct and honest. That included admitting that I did believe sufficiently in the providence of God to the extent of giving him control of everything. My 'Yes' would be a 'Yes'; my 'No' would be a genuine 'No'. Faced with a lack of clarity, my answer was different: I ran into the darkness.

Now it wasn't that I fled from the *gringo* and his message in order to plan the next prank in the dormitory. Such thoughts were far from me, but I did understand the seriousness of the moment, and maybe that explains the distress

I felt in my heart when I heard those extreme appeals. Today I realise that it is possible that what I have just written describes the heart of someone with little faith in God and who blames his own unbelief on others, whether people or situations. Perhaps that is what was happening. I do know for certain, though, that decisions about my mission in the Kingdom of God that I could have taken in my youth were put off until much later. I lost so much time, I tell myself now. Many plans were put off, and later could no longer be realised, for my life was already mapped out as far as work, family and church were concerned.

I am convinced that the subject of one's personal mission is not limited to a specific age-group. However, it's common knowledge, both inside and outside the church, that the so-called 'impossible' missionary assignments are for young people whose energy and idealism are fascinated by the challenges involved. With the same boldness with which the young plan to conquer the world, they take on the challenge of conquering it for Christ. This is the reason I regret my delays in this area, and I write these personal reflections, thinking of the young people, and maybe also parents and leaders, who will read them.

I conclude this introduction with a question: could it be that I was the only one to feel uncomfortable with sermons about only one tiny aspect of the truth – as if a whole *samba* could be composed using only one musical note? Had those messages reached my heart by a less narrow and more biblical route, perhaps I would not have spent so much time travelling off-road instead of staying on the highway. If there is any truth in what I am saying, it doesn't have to be this way. We can still learn from these experiences (and from others that are ongoing) and change what needs to be changed. How? Well, let's proceed, starting with the dreaded *Go into all the world*, my cue for fleeing from the campfire meeting.

2. Go into All the World

It is impossible to escape the fact that every translation implies interpretation. And what a difference a translation makes – or, in my case at least, it could have made a difference.

In addition to the Lord's call to Isaiah mentioned in the previous chapter, Mark 16:15 also had a strong presence in my youth (and still is special to me): *he said to them, Go into all the world and preach the gospel to all creation*. In Matthew's account, the wording of the so-called 'Great Commission' is: *Go and make disciples of all nations, baptising them in the name of the Father and of the Son and of the Holy Spirit, and teaching them to obey everything I have commanded you. And surely I am with you always, to the very end of the age* (Matthew 28:19-20).

While I am convinced that 'go' is the best translation, a literal translation in these verses would be 'going' or even 'having gone'. This is because the emphasis of Jesus' commandment is that *the gospel be preached to every creature* or, as in Matthew's version, that we *make disciples of all nations*. But I can see that to translate the Greek as 'going' or 'having gone', while still giving the idea of movement, actually weakens the notion that Jesus is 'sending' his disciples. The translation 'Go', on the other hand, affirms this strongly.

So I agree with the translation. What's the problem then? The problem is that the word 'Go' has become the focus of the sentence, to the detriment of the original meaning ('going' and 'having gone'). It may seem a small difference, but in my youth it was dramatic, for it *diminishes* the idea that Jesus was commanding us to preach the gospel, that is, to make disciples, and it *encourages* the idea that we must go to a particular place. Hence the favourite song of the worship time round the campfire: 'I will go, Lord /I will obey you.' The logic, while misinterpreted, was actually very simple: If I 'go', I cannot stay.

Now this interpretation has a geographical dimension, as evidenced in Jesus' own command, for he added *into all the world*. It seems to me that a subtle distortion has come into being, the result of a desire to simplify issues, and born out of genuine missionary fervour – namely, that in order to obey Jesus' command you must leave the place where you are and travel far away. The further away we are, the more obedient we will be. And if we cannot go we send someone else. So the problem is solved, for it is not possible for every one to go because some one needs to stay behind to provide spiritual and material support for those who go (something never mentioned in the worship times round the campfire because it weakens the 'Go!').

So there it is: the concept of 'mission' as it was passed on to me. And I consider it to be at the very least incomplete, if not distorted. At this point it is important to say that I know people who treat these concepts with great care because they understand that what is at stake is not just recruitment of soldiers to be sent: they value faithfulness to the Word, so they teach with precision the things I have just commented on. Even so, there remains a widely held misconception that 'missions' and 'mission' are not really the same thing. The first word involves the 'Go'; the second does not. The first involves selling the furniture, the refrigerator and leaving everything behind; the second does not. The first is the concern of the church's missions department; the second is not.

It is not easy to detect any command to a 'Go to here, to where you are' in the well-known words of Jesus. That would be absurd, at the very least a linguistic error. But my impression is that to translate 'Go' as 'Going' or 'Having gone' would facilitate the inclusion of our condominium, neighbourhood, school, workplace – or even our church – as places for missionary endeavour. Such a translation does not reinforce the imperative of geographical displacement; rather, the emphasis is on preaching and making disciples in the very place to which we have gone and where we have settled down.

I would summarise what I wish I'd learned in my youth in the following terms: *Jesus commissions us to preach the gospel and to make disciples; do that wherever you are, be it in your* home *city (Jerusalem) or wherever you end up living. If you feel a specific call to some distant place, obey, because God needs witnesses to the ends of the earth.*

I believe that hearing those words would not have forced me to flee into the darkness of the bush during the camp altar calls. Maybe my teenage zeal would have led me to hear a call to be a witness at home, in the neighbourhood, at school, in the church, among my wider family. Maybe I would have concluded that, to heed such a call, I would need some preparation in order to better understand the nature of this mission field. Maybe then, on my knees and despairingly, I would have sought the power of God, seeking the charismatic gifts, the anointing, in order to be able to play a minimal part in this most noble mission.

3. The Heart of the Onion

The idea of peeling the onion to see what is inside (and the tears that accompany such research) can be a good metaphor for the research that precedes the visit to the missionary factory. It can lead us to those philosophical questions about the origin of everything. Questions such as: 'What was there before the factory?' Is that just a fun question – laugh, change the subject, and no harm caused? In fact, I want to suggest that the missionary factory is not the heart of the onion at all, that there is another layer to be removed before we get there. The fact is that the whole idea of mission has its origin in eternity. It's not our thing, but God's.

I would like to invite you to peel the 'onion of the incarnation' to discover what is inside it, the composition of its twin centre. I think it is possible (and necessary) to go deeper than the '10/40 Window' concept, than the various Lausanne Conferences, than World Vision, than national missionary agencies, missionary training colleges or local churches. Behind and before all this amazing organisational structure we discover, as John the evangelist explains, the heart of a Father willing to give himself, and the heart of a Son willing to 'go', to become incarnate. *For God so loved the world that he gave his one and only Son, that whoever believes in him shall not perish but have eternal life* (John 3:16).

Yes, at the heart of the onion lies the loving heart of God who wants to speak to us by means of his Son (Hebrews 1:1). Here, in all its splendour, is the twin centre of the missionary onion:

1. A Father's heart of love which is prepared to sacrifice, and
2. A concrete gesture of renunciation which gives up rights to glory and pitches a tent among us.

Put simply, the motive is *love* and the action is the *incarnation*. That's the model, and from it we develop our motivations, methods and actions. The incarnation is the model for mission, set out by God himself. To understand this clearly could be our starting-point for thinking more realistically about our own situation.

In trying to penetrate the thinking of the Father and the Son, we discover that all that they did was done out of love. They owed us nothing and they had no need of us at all. All they wanted was our love. This suggests that they were not obliged to do what they did. It was a gesture both sacrificial and voluntary. In the words of the composer Guilherme Kerr, 'No-one could make him do it / It was his own love that moved him / That is why he is King.'

It reminds me of Peter's second and definitive missionary call which came after the dramas around Jesus' crucifixion: Peter's cowardice, his betrayal, that look from the Master, the rooster crowing, the return to Capernaum and to fishing, the unsuccessful fishing trip, a second attempt and an amazing catch, 'It's him!' Then the fish on the coals and the resurrected Lord asking, *'Simon son of John, do you truly love me more than these?'* '*Yes, Lord,'* he answered, '*Yes, Lord, you know that I love you.'* Jesus said, '*Feed my lambs'* (John 21:15).

Peter was not told to *Go!* He was sent on a pastoral mission. Almost a command to *Stay!* the bottom line being '*if you do not have love, you are nothing'* (1 Corinthians 13:2). Love is the motivating force for any action in the Kingdom of God. That is the Ground Zero marker of mission.

Once again, the conclusions of our research point to modest, humble and anonymous things. I am thinking of ordinary everyday life in 'Jerusalem', and recall the problems that arise when a church doesn't understand this Ground Zero marker. There's the guitarist in a bad mood, the Sunday School teacher who never stops complaining, the deacon who moans, 'Somebody needs to fix things round here', and the worship leader who thinks he is a celebrity in control of large crowds, etc. Such situations demand that Jesus' question be repeated: 'Do you love me? Well, do my work with joy and thanksgiving.' And I would add that, if we can't do it that way, it would probably be better to stop, for what we are doing is not mission. It is something else as yet undefined.

Because we are accustomed to understanding missions as something big, important, distant and intangible, we do not realise that personal sacrificial love is fundamental. But let's not deceive ourselves. Everyone will hear the question, full-time missionaries too – in fact, every individual soul: 'What's your motivation? Why are you here, so far away from your home? Is it for love of me and of these for whom I died?' In any case, it should be clear to all of us that, even when thinking of those whose results are considered satisfactory by churches and mission boards, nothing is of any value unless it is done in love. Let no-one deceive himself in this regard.

Once I inadvertently overheard a pastor tell a fellow Christian: 'If you are suffering so much, if you are so upset, if everybody is wrong, why continue? Let someone else do it; God doesn't need your complaining. Serve with joy.' And I thought to myself: He's right. Suffering is inevitable in any project that calls for self-sacrifice; but this type of suffering, as of one bearing a heavy burden, is not inevitable in the work of the Kingdom. Service motivated by love is notable for its joy. Therefore fear, need, lack of alternative work opportunities, family pressures and so on are not worthy reasons for becoming involved in this ministry. Without the mainspring of love, no ministry will exemplify the incarnation model.

I know that such an argument is a simplification, that in most cases our motives compete with each other in a complex way. Worse still, they include conscious and unconscious elements, be they admitted or not, legitimate or not. And only the Lord himself is able to discern some of our motives, for they are so complicated that judgement by an outsider would be an act of irresponsibility. It is a matter to be discerned privately, alone in one's room with the Lord who sees in secret. But, whatever the scenario, if the answer does not come from above, we run the risk of launching out on an adventure whose end is uncertain. To be clear, this is equally true, whether for a motivation to say 'Yes' or to say 'No'. The Ground Zero marker is the pre-condition for personal fulfilment, within the will of God.

The words of the pastoral rebuke I mentioned call us back to the question of the *Cross*, whether in its literal sense or as a metaphor for renunciation. Incarnation means giving up a peaceful life, our comfort, our reasons not to do something, in short, giving up our own 'glory'. More than that, incarnation is a process of *identification* associated with *renunciation*.

Identification is a very personal psychological mechanism by which we put ourselves inside another's skin, situation or need. We identify more easily with situations we ourselves have experienced, with people who suffer from a pain that we know, or who have a weakness or strength, an ability or disability, that we also detect in ourselves. The phenomenon is called *isomorphism*, meaning that it has a similar form. Perhaps that's why Christ became incarnate – in order to experience our pain, our problems. As a result, he became a merciful and faithful High Priest, for he is able to have compassion on our pains, having personally experienced all of them and with great intensity. He is merciful in that he suffered. He identified himself with our sad condition.

The Cross also means that, without renunciation, without choosing to serve, there is no way to be a witness to Christ and no way to reproduce his model among us. To be incarnate is to give up our own glory, whatever that means for each one. Another detail to consider: renunciation, when done out of love, does not need stimuli such as fear, threats, prestige, defined roles, vanity, recognition or other elements so prevalent in human structures. Renunciation is voluntary, sacrificial, and often completely anonymous.

It could also be said that renunciation is intimate and personal. Although in no way comparable, it is like suicide in that no-one can do it for another. Therefore, if someone wants to 'renounce' your tithe to finance the work; or 'renounce' your comfort so that you can take on a task; or your rest time in order that a group may meet – be very wary. Either something comes from your heart and is motivated by love or you don't own it. Ask such people to give up what *they* hold dear. That will be pleasing to God.

Incarnation is continual renunciation; it's a lifestyle, a discipline with no end date, for you will practise it until the end of your life, and find in it your rewards and joys. Yes, I do mean rewards and joys. Your deliberate, rational renunciation will be a source of great happiness, unspeakable joy and fulfilment for your soul. Let's believe that. Only those who have had the experience know these true riches.

Incarnation is the way to exercise the ministry of reconciliation (2 Corinthians 5:18), for Jesus' example is prescriptive for both missionary *method* and missionary *attitude*. So incarnation is identification in the sense of treating everyone in the same way, so that power (even the power to make good things happen) gives way to a love that controls nothing (for love and control are incompatible), and the desire to be served gives way to the desire to serve, a desire at once voluntary, kind, considerate, creative and anonymous. In fact, in most cases, only our Lord will know what we have actually done. And he will also know that it was done out of love for him. That is enough. *God is not unjust; he will not forget your work and the love you have shown him as you have helped his people and continue to help them* (Hebrews 6:10).

By means of Jesus' incarnation, the thunderous, avenging deity appears as the sheep destined for slaughter; the long-awaited great king turns up as a suffering servant determined to experience the pains of the human condition – but not our sin. He is not proud for he does not see himself better than anyone; he is not selfish for he does not keep to himself or hide the good he has received; he is not arrogant nor even a judge for he did not come to judge the world but to proclaim *the acceptable day of salvation*.

Incarnation is even more: it is the perfection of communication. We will devote a chapter to the theme but, for now, I leave you with the following text which will be our inspiration: *In the past God spoke to our forefathers through the prophets at many times and in various ways, but in these last days he has spoken to us by his Son, whom he appointed heir of all things, and through whom he made the universe* (Hebrews 1:1-2).

Put succinctly, *incarnation is to be born into the world of another person, to place yourself alongside them with a view to helping them return to the Father*. In this context, 'to be born' means just what it means at Christmas, starting off small and vulnerable in order to learn about the everyday concerns, the motives and circumstances of others. It is to identify, to develop mercy.

'Born into the world', into a fallen world marked by pain, all sorts of problems, different age-groups, joys, dangers, gifts, dreams, fears and everything that makes up the consciousness of the other person. Following the order of the definition above, 'another' can mean people groups, races, nations, a particular country or city, a place of work, a school, our personal relationships, church, family, spouse, children or parents.

'Alongside' means no paternalism. Whoever does something for another does it without that person's involvement; incarnation, on the other hand, is concerned about maturity and chooses to walk with the other towards the goals of submissive autonomy and fruitfulness. 'To return to the Father' means to be reconciled to God; it means salvation; it means discipleship (*teaching them to obey everything I have commanded you*, Matthew 28:20).

How Is a Missionary Born?

Returning to the illustration of the onion, there at the very centre, right next to God's heart, we find a soul that is beginning to beat at the same frequency, with the same pulse rate as God's; that is touched with the same inexplicable impulse to reconcile; that is infected by the same spontaneous and sacrificial love; that burns with the same desire to overcome barriers (because to incarnate is to overcome immense barriers and obstacles) and to search after others; that is willing to set itself apart by joining a special 'Order' (the 'Order' of those who wash others' feet); and that serves in the 'Order', right from the initial reception of a life-mission to reconcile the world to God. In this intimate and holy place, the soul hears God's voice saying:

You are a chosen people, a royal priesthood, a holy nation, a people belonging to God, that you may declare the praises of him who called you out of darkness into his wonderful light (1 Peter 2:9). So go and do what has been done for you; forgive as you have been forgiven; serve as you have been served; teach as you have been taught; make disciples as you were made a disciple; love as you have been loved. Now that you are my missionary, exercise your mission in this total way – not forgetting to do all it with the attitude of *Christ Jesus your Lord who, being in very nature God, did not consider equality with God something to be grasped, but made himself nothing, taking the very nature of a servant... he humbled himself and became obedient to death* (Philippians 2:6-7). Your methods and your attitudes must be those of your incarnate Lord.'

So be born into the world of your children; into the world of your spouse; into the world of your fellow Christians; into the world of your church. Don't be an epiphany, an apparition that appears from time to time in Sunday School classes, ministry and worship teams. Rather, serve everyone in every way you can; don't expect to be served but learn to serve willingly; learn to be useful in the tiniest things, even in small and less noble things; don't wait for an adequate infrastructure, a special role, for things to improve, for someone else to do something. Serve! Do it with joy in your heart and thanksgiving on your lips.

In other words, don't be a visitor, whether in your home, church or ministry teams. Rather, decide to be born into these worlds, identifying with them and practising that renunciation which involves doing tasks you dislike even before they ask you. This is what it is to advance God's Kingdom in the best way you can and with love as your only motive.

And I promise you that you will be in no way inferior to those whom I send to *Judea and Samaria, and to the ends of the earth.* Neither will you feel humbled by them, for they are your fellow workers and, if they are where they are, it is because you are faithful to me here, in Jerusalem.

It's time to move on to another subject, but I leave it to you, my reader, to think more about these things.

One last word though. Do you know why I think so much about Jerusalem? It's because if I were the enemy and wanted to wipe good missionaries off the face of the earth in a few generations, I wouldn't persecute them only on their mission fields by making their life difficult even to the point of turning it into a hell – if that were possible. I would attack the missionary factory by giving parents, whether biological or spiritual, lots of work and lots of *mammon.* In that way, they would be unable to concentrate on their personal mission responsibilities. I would suggest to them that they have a great need of comfort, entertainment and fun. As a result, they would become careless, distracted, demanding consumers and psychologically obese; their children would not have family worship times or Bible instruction or even the physical presence or example of parents; regular church attendance would be denied the children (my strategy means that parent-missionaries would be too tired after late nights on Saturdays), for parents would want to stay in bed longer on a Sunday morning. Simple things not even classed as sins, 'just' the normal pressures and pleasures of modern life.

To render them psychologically obese, I would suggest to them a slight twist in the fashionable concept of self-esteem, persuading them to give excess attention to themselves and develop a subtle fixation on their personal needs. The correct word is selfishness, but I wouldn't use it, for to do so would betray my real intentions. The technique is that, under the excuse of 'love yourself in order to be able to love others', I would lead them away from any proper understanding of the meaning of Christian service. They would then spend the rest of their lives in pursuit of personal satisfaction. If possible, I would make them resentful for not receiving satisfaction from God.

Once the culture of self-esteem has been rooted in an individual, it's easy to work on smaller issues like grudges, murmurings, disagreements, factions, fatigue, lack of enthusiasm, etc. In other words, it's easy to breed the anti-mission germ in somebody's soul and then pass it on to children as their inheritance.

Yes, I would sabotage the true awareness of the mission that each one has in and to their own Jerusalem, and so destroy the basic values centred on family and church, the apple of God's eye. In a few generations, the factory would no longer produce its own missionaries; they would all be outsourced – with the exception of some crippled ones rescued by God from the flames of our cities and who are no longer asleep. Thank God for them.

You didn't get the allusion to crippled ones? Not to worry. I wrote about this elsewhere[4] and include part of the text here:

Alone in his room, that ordinary soul – a mother, a father, a son, a member of the church – will hear the Father say: 'Go! Offer up what I have given you; forgive as I have forgiven you; minister to others as I have ministered to you; teach what I taught you; make disciples as you were made a disciple; love as I have loved you. In this way, you will leave this room with your life mission, your 'Jerusalem mission'. Fulfil this mission with the motivation and method of one who cares and gets close to others – that is, with love and incarnation.

'If you are willing to assist me to reconcile to myself your spouse and children, your parents, friends and brothers in Christ, I will make you my missionary. You will receive power from the Holy Spirit for this. You will be my witness in your home, church and workplace. In the heavenly realms you will have the status of a minister. And, from the starting-point of this, your faithfulness, I will be able to choose sons and daughters of yours and send them to the ends of the earth. And wherever they are, they will be proud to say, "I know how to build up the apple of God's eye – whether it be a family or a church – for I lived it out at home. My parents taught me."'

4. The Missionary Call

We concluded the previous chapter by comparing our children with what I call 'cripples rescued by God from among the flames of our cities' – an allusion to Zechariah 3:2. This is not prejudice, let alone disdain for those who have not been brought up in the church. More than once, I have found myself arriving, new and unknown, in a new city and church, simply because of a change of job. So I would like to develop this idea and then describe the typical journey from missionary call to arrival on the 'mission field' and the start of ministry. Hopefully, my description of what is typical or average will help us to look at ourselves and appreciate the inevitable differences that arise.

I have already told you about the worship time round the campfire and return to the theme, not now to describe a personal experience, but rather as a metaphor for the first call, the first appeal, the first awareness of vocation. Yes, it all begins with a call, God's call. And it is not always discerned immediately. There are many reports of people commissioned and approved by God who say, 'I didn't realise that God was calling me to this; something special had to happen for me to get to this point.'

An even more delicate situation arises when the call is to go somewhere near home, to our Jerusalem. Perhaps because we have no appropriate liturgical formalities like the appeal made round the campfire, no ostensible mission structures and nothing corresponding to events such as the missionary marathons of preaching and fund-raising, complete with missionaries from afar who appear each October, this call can be disguised under the cloak of 'a call to consecration'. While not belittling that important aspect of Christian experience, it is a fact that, strictly speaking, all teaching about 'Mission Jerusalem' could be included under the title 'Christian life'. In theological faculties and seminaries, they are generally treated as distinct topics, separate from missions, even in different departments.

This observation is necessary in order to avoid the conclusion that nothing is taught about mission to those near home (or 'intromission'). On the contrary, all the themes (and many more) that concern us in this book are covered in some detail in courses on the Christian life. But in my view, the teaching given puts no emphasis on a specific call. It is as if personal consecration to live the multiple challenges of the Christian life did not include a missionary call. This omission is the fruit of the notion that it is not appropriate to speak of a call, not to 'Go!' but to stay near home.

Because of this disservice done to teaching on the Christian life, I propose a fusion of contents and methods. On the one hand, when the missionary reaches their 'mission field', they will live a normal Christian life among those to whom they have been sent. In addition, when the experience is cross-cultural, there is a strong element of proclamation. It's as though there isn't much room for timidity or self-examination. Quite so – it's very clear to that missionary that their light must not be hidden *under a bowl* (Matthew 5:14).

However, when the call is to work near home, the element of proclamation is not always taken into account. Why is that? In my opinion, there is a lack of understanding of that specific call, and therefore no preparation or commissioning for it. Yes, the *Go!* is loud and clear, and it's usual for the serious believer to be careful in his Christian walk and personal devotional life. But it is not so common for him to realise that there is an element of proclamation in his walk with God, that making disciples of all nations by *teaching them to keep all the words I have taught you* is also part of the package. Such an understanding would become much clearer if believers were aware of having received a clear call such as is common in the context of missions to distant places.

The concept of a clear and unmistakable call immediately reminds us of Paul's call on the road to Damascus, and Jesus' call of the apostles. I have chosen to look at another one, the call of Moses, and his circumstances, to draw out some lessons that apply both to those sent to the ends of the earth and those sent to their Jerusalem. I will offer five observations about the text of Exodus 3:1-20:

> *Moses was tending the flock of Jethro his father-in-law, the priest of Midian, and he led the flock to the far side of the wilderness and came to Horeb, the mountain of God. There the angel of the Lord appeared to him in flames of fire from within a bush. Moses saw that though the bush was on fire it did not burn up.* So Moses thought, *'I will go over and see this strange sight – why the bush does not burn up'.* When the Lord saw that he had gone over to look, God called to him from within the bush, *'Moses! Moses!' And Moses said, 'Here I am.' 'Do not come any closer,'* God said. *'Take off your sandals, for the place where you are standing is holy ground.'* Then he said, *'I am the God of your father, the God of Abraham, the God of Isaac and the God of Jacob.'* At this, Moses hid his face, because he was afraid to look at God. The LORD said, *'I have indeed seen the misery of my people in Egypt. I have heard them crying out because of their slave drivers, and am concerned about their suffering.* So *I have come down to rescue them from the hand of the Egyptians and to bring them up out of that land into a good and spacious land, a land flowing with milk and honey – the home of the Canaanites, Hittites, Amorites, Perizzites, Hivites and Jebusites.* And now *the cry of the Israelites has reached me, and I have seen the way the Egyptians are oppressing them. So now, go. I am sending you to Pharaoh to bring my people, the Israelites, out of Egypt.'* But *Moses said to God, 'Who am I, that I should go to Pharaoh and bring the Israelites out of Egypt?'* And *God said, 'I will be with you. And this will be the sign to you that it is I who have sent you: when you have brought the people out of Egypt, you will worship God on this mountain'. Moses said to God, 'Suppose I go to Israelites and say unto them, "The God of your fathers has sent me to you," and they ask me, "What is his name?"* Then *what shall I tell them?' God said to Moses, 'I AM WHO I AM. This is what you are to say to the Israelites, "I AM has sent me to you".'* God also said to Moses, *'Say to the Israelites, "The LORD, the God of your fathers – the God of Abraham, the God of*

Isaac and the God of Jacob – has sent me to you." This is my name for ever, the name by which I am to be remembered from generation to generation. Go, assemble the elders of Israel and say to them, 'The LORD, the God of your fathers – the God of Abraham, the God of Isaac and Jacob – appeared to me and said: "I have watched over you and have seen what has been done to you in Egypt. And I have promised to bring you up out of your misery in Egypt into the land of the Canaanites, Hittites, Amorites, Perizzites, Hivites and Jebusites – a land flowing with milk and honey." The elders of Israel will listen to you. Then you and the elders will go to the king of Egypt and say to him, "The LORD, the God of the Hebrews, hath met with us. Let us take a three-day journey into the wilderness to offer sacrifices to the LORD our God." But I know that the king of Egypt will not let you go unless a mighty hand compels him. So I will stretch out my hand and strike the Egyptians with all the wonders that I perform among them. After that, he will let you go.'

Go to My People

1. The first fact that strikes me about the account of Moses' call is that it included a historical dimension which, even if not always fully perceived by the actors involved, was planned by God, used by him for his purposes, and over which he exercises control. Chapters 1 and 2 of Exodus, and particularly 2:23-25, tell us that God was at work in history to forge a people in whom (and to whom) he would reveal himself, and through whom he would carry forward the covenants he had made with people who were no longer there, or not yet there. God was at work long before Moses became aware of his role in that history. Likewise, we too begin to understand things when God decides that the time has come for him to reveal to us that he is going to intervene in history.

This helps us to understand that God does not call us without having some purpose in mind, that he does not call us for ourselves alone. In fact, when we begin to hear his call, we are already caught up in a web of events that go far beyond our limited understanding of them. The consequences of our participation in God's plans extend to the past and to the future, to places near at hand and far away. An interesting aside as far as our general theme is concerned: Moses did not receive a *'Go to the ends of the earth'* call. He was more like Jesus who, on His incarnation, was sent to his own people. And, like Jesus, *he came to that which was his own. Yet to all who received Him...* (John 1:11). I stop there, for I am sure you can guess where my argument is leading.

Moses' greatness can work against the lesson we need to learn here. We can be tempted to think that this is not our case; that we are not contributing to anyone's history; that we do not even need a call. Let's not deceive ourselves. We know nothing of the history God is writing all around us, whether the history of our own lives, our family, church, city, or even of the future. In this respect, I find comfort in biblical genealogies when I discover there the name of an ordinary person whose only claim to fame is that he was somebody's ancestor. And this 'somebody' went on to be used by God to mark the history of God's people. We just don't know how God will use us. But *he* knows.

2. The second fact to note in Moses' call is that, normally, the process by means of which a missionary is called is part of a journey of humiliation and brokenness. Before his call, Moses was a prince in Egypt and accustomed to palace life, a very different world from the modest circumstances described in Exodus 3:1. He was reduced to being a shepherd in charge of his father-in-law's sheep, a situation of subordination and humiliation. God acted in the same way with Paul, when he put him under the tutelage of the unknown Ananias and then of Barnabas. The fact that God dealt with his own Son in similar fashion (see Isaiah 53 and Philippians 2) leads to the conclusion that this is God's definitive method. The lesson is so clear that, in Deuteronomy, we find Moses passing on his experience to the Israelites as if to state that their pilgrimage and humiliation were a replay of Moses' consciousness of his own mission.

> *Remember how the LORD your God led you all the way in the wilderness these forty years, to humble you and to test you in order to know what was in your heart, whether or not you would keep his commands. He humbled you, causing you to hunger and then feeding you with manna, which neither you nor your ancestors had known, to teach you that man does not live on bread alone but on every word that comes out of the mouth of the LORD* (Deuteronomy 8:2-3).

This aspect of God's call merits further consideration. Our calling does not necessarily have to come with prestige, whether derived from formal roles or from social recognition. If such is our precondition for service – if we are counting on possessions or on ordination; on a large desk in an air-conditioned room; on a call that causes no rupture in our circumstances – we need to review the experience carefully. It may have been a call from men, or even no call at all. And if we find that we are unwilling for our heart to be broken, that we are not in fact malleable clay in God's hands, then we most certainly will be of no use to God and his purposes. At this point, a word of consolation and hope is in order. If we're already worn out and impatient with ourselves, let's remember that God spent forty years preparing Moses, and could take the same amount time with us. For this reason, it is important to recognise, value and honour the Jethros, Ananiases and Barnabases God sends into our lives – to teach us how to go about the mission he has purposed for us.

3. The third fact to note is that an experience of this nature stresses what is an apparently trivial lesson – namely, that a missionary career begins with a call from God. To the missionary sent to the ends of the earth, this clear call is as necessary as it is common. The reason is simple: few are willing to risk taking on such an enormous task without an unmistakable awareness of call, and that awareness itself requires time to reach maturity. The period of preparation, the financial resources involved, setting up the necessary infrastructure and planning the strategies to be adopted on the 'field'– all these things guarantee that there is time for maturation, whether it be of the missionary's own heart, or that of his family or church. When missionaries eventually set out, they leave behind a large rearguard of many people committed to their mission and their support – people who in a secondary way have also heard their call. This phenomenon is necessary and healthy, since it creates a network of support and protection for the missionaries and, at the same time, a network of prayer and interest, so that the missionaries don't feel lonely as though sent off to fend for themselves. However, all of this is not enough to prevent the doubts, crises and uncertainties that arise from the day-to-day struggles of life. These crises become even more devastating when the awareness of a call does not exist or is lost, or when there are doubts about whether it was from God in the first place.

Moses must have had frequent attacks of doubt, but in those times he had a moment of call to return to, for the burning bush still burned in his memory and had the effect of making his encounter with God unmistakable and unforgettable: *Moses! Moses!* The very words gave him the strength to carry on. He was certain that it was God who had called him to his mission. Perhaps that was the purpose of the supernatural phenomenon of the bush that had burned and was not consumed. Moses knew that that moment in time and the place itself were holy, set apart and never trivialised by Moses throughout his career (Exodus 3:5).

To the missionary sent to Jerusalem today, this essential element of mission, God's clear, unmistakable call, can seem almost imperceptible, in spite of the fact that it brings strength and comfort in those times of weariness and bewilderment which follow persecution, misunderstandings, doubts and so many other battles faced by contemporary Christians.

Every missionary must have a call. For example, a father trying to bring up his child *in the training and instruction of the Lord* (Ephesians 6:4) will need this awareness of his call and, in prayer, will seek strength and discernment for the difficult times ahead. He will face situations where he will have to decide between obeying the Word or following the advice of the world, occasions when he will have to sacrifice his own comfort, time and convenience to carry out his ministry as a parent.

My prayer is that this understanding of what constitutes a call becomes part of a missionary revival among Brazilian evangelicals. That, when asked, 'What are you doing for God?' (meaning 'What about your call to *Go*? What are you doing so near home?'), a mother or father will reply with conviction and zeal, 'I've been called to exercise the ministry of parenting my children for the next few years and, given the importance of that mission field, God has asked me to give all my time to it.' And may each parent prepare himself or herself for this mission, praying, reading and choosing material for family worship times. Add to the list fun times, bedtime stories, videos, playing games, family stories, and stories about role models and heroes – and everything else that the creativity of a parent with a missionary heart is capable of inventing – for the sole purpose of teaching a child to love the Lord with all their heart, soul and strength (Deuteronomy 6:5), and that from an early age.

4. The fourth fact we observe in this passage is that a missionary's call becomes a reality when he or she perceives God's plans and then incorporates them into his or her own dreams. In Exodus 3:7-9 we find God sharing with Moses his vision of history and his redemptive intentions.

> *The LORD said, 'I have indeed seen the misery of my people in Egypt. I have heard them crying out because of their slave drivers,* and am concerned about their *suffering. So I have come down to rescue them from the hand of the Egyptians and to bring them up out of that land into a good and spacious land, a land flowing with milk and honey... And now the cry of the Israelites has reached me, and I have seen the way the Egyptians are oppressing them'* (Exodus 3:7-9).

It was an unusual moment in Moses' life, and, as I understand it, the message for us is that, without this understanding and vision, there can be no spiritual mission. The genuine missionary is the one to whom God reveals what he sees and what he intends to do – even if he does that by means of a simple diagnosis of the reality on the ground. A strategic, panoramic vision of the mission to be accomplished is important, as it both motivates the missionary and helps them to make correct decisions. Better still, when spouses and children have the same vision burning in their hearts, the whole understanding of mission is intensified and strengthened. The way ahead becomes clearer, even though there may be some uncertainty as to details. The need for discernment is a constant.

Often this vision reaches the missionary's heart quite simply: they already have a specific type of missionary activity on their heart. They might know an agency specialising in work with children, Indian tribes, people from the East, or those who live on the outskirts of large cities, and they identify with their vision and purpose. In other cases, the missionary is moved by a presentation where existing, well-structured challenges are laid out. Even then, there is much that is personal in the decisions to be taken and not a little anxiety until each one is sure that their dreams are indeed God's plans.

This seems to me to be the normal process, but I am concerned that this phenomenon is a lot more vague in the case of 'local' missionaries – for example, ordinary church members, Sunday School teachers, folk with secular jobs, young couples. Without a clear perception of the strategic and historical purpose in their regular activities, believers who really want to serve are left without guidelines. This lack of structuring of the 'mission to Jerusalem' within the local church also leaves the individual without institutional reference points that could help. Thus there is a need for appropriate missionary strategies linked to the 'call to Jerusalem', and for motivating, inspiring, instructing, training, sending and accompanying the missionaries called to work there. (We will consider these strategy issues in the final chapter.)

5. Our fifth observation from Exodus 3 is that Moses' experience of call teaches us that, when God wants to act in history, he usually does it through people he calls, enables and sends: a missionary is one who attends to God's call to act in history. Verse 10 gives us to understand that Moses was shocked when he realised that everything God had just said he would do would involve his, Moses', participation; that God's method of using people would be set in motion in his own life; that God's intervention in the world of humanity involves people.

God does not change people and their stories from a distance, and the close proximity required was fully realised in the incarnation of the Word. God calls men and women into a relationship with himself, to converse with him, to reason, discuss and enter into a covenant where his desire is to put all his cards on the table. In the language of the father of the 'prodigal son', *Everything I have is yours. But we had to celebrate and be glad, because this brother of yours was dead and is alive again; he was lost and is found* (Luke 15:31-32).

It is through people that God reaches other people and works in their lives. Therefore we should not expect him to act in a situation that we are praying about, when he has already shown us his diagnosis and the way forward. We should not just sit and wait for God to do something, or even hope that somebody, somewhere, will do something about the problem. It may be that all the elements of a missionary call are already on our heart, but that we are not taking into account the possibility that the call really has been addressed to us.

If God has shared his plans with us, it may be that he is waiting for us to understand that we are the ones being sent into a particular situation. For example, Nehemiah prayed for three months for the restoration of Jerusalem, even though he was in captivity and cupbearer to the conquering king. At a specific moment in time, he realised that the mission was his and, prepared and ready, presented himself to the king. It's disconcerting, so we wonder, 'Who am I, for such a mission?' That was Moses' question. And we tend to identify with this man who had a fright when the Lord presented him with his mission (Exodus 3:11). How deceitful our heart is! One minute I see myself as a great leader who will be mentioned in history books and genealogies and, as a result, I fail to discern my little, local mission. Next minute, faced with this important mission, I feel too small for the task.

Notice that the question, *Who am I?* has gone unanswered. God could have said, 'You are Moses! Don't put yourself down. You deserve this mission; I see great qualities in you.' Rather, God chose to say, 'It doesn't matter. What matters is that I will be with you.' This affirmation from the Most High really comforts me because I realise that *it does not, therefore, depend on man's desire or effort, but on God's mercy* (Romans 9:16). *Not that we are competent in ourselves to claim anything for ourselves, but our competence comes from God* (2 Corinthians 3:5). It is worth emphasising that no-one is fit for missionary work. Hence the brokenness and humiliation that mark its beginning. The Lord must prepare us, therefore let's not be intimidated when we hear his voice.

On the other hand, if we find that our mission is too burdensome for us, we need to know that we are not the ones who define its success or failure: rather, it depends more on our being teachable. Even if it looks as though we're coming to a sad end, as happened with Moses who could not enter the

Promised Land, God's presence will help us say with dignity, as he did: *He is your praise; he is your God, who performed for you those great and awesome wonders you saw with your own eyes* (Deuteronomy 10:21).

Some final thoughts will comfort our hearts. First, it is God who gives us those who will hear us: *The elders of Israel will listen to you* (Exodus 3:18). On many occasions, I needed to hear those simple words when dealing with a rebellious teenager. And I can well imagine that this was the verse on my mother's bedside table. So let's trust that it is God who speaks to the heart, and not us, and that his gentle voice reaches right inside to the division between soul and spirit.

Second, it is God who enables those he calls: *What is that in your hand?* (Exodus 4:2). The skills and competencies for missionary work will come from God himself, and while I despise neither academic training nor in-service training, the qualifications of the heart that are essential to mission are found only in him.

Third, it is comforting to know that, in one way or another, God will make up for any shortcomings we may have: *I know he can speak well* (Exodus 4:14). Amen.

May Moses' call be the starting-point for those who dream the Lord's dreams for their people.

5. The Ministry of Reconciliation

'All this is from God, who reconciled us to himself through Christ and gave us the ministry of reconciliation: that God was reconciling the world to himself in Christ, not counting men's sins against them. And he has committed to us the message of reconciliation. We are therefore Christ's ambassadors, as though God were making his appeal through us' (2 Corinthians 5:18-20).

To return to the idea of peeling the missionary onion, we might say that there is an outer skin that covers the call of God. We have already reflected on the starting-point of everything as far as mission is concerned: what I call the double core of the onion is made up of a fatherly heart that loves sacrificially, along with a dynamic whereby that fatherly heart of God abandons its own comfort and glory and becomes incarnate, pitching its tent among those it desires to save. This is our model, the motive power behind ministry.

Following on from that, we reflected on the first layer of skin that covers this core – namely, that the God who calls us to salvation is searching for fellow workers in his worldwide mission. The next layer speaks of the nature of mission, but not in relation to the tasks to be performed. In fact, this aspect doesn't interest me very much – for the one who loves will always find a way to act. (We will, however, examine some practical aspects later when we look at lessons to be learned from Jesus as he washed the disciples' feet.) Love is the chief lesson of the Parable of the Good Samaritan. The doctor of the Law, bound as he was by rules and regulations, was unable to help the needy man lying by the side of the road because he didn't love him. But the Samaritan, out of love, found a way to save the needy man even though his actions involved breaking rules and protocols.

So, leaving aside the question about *what* to do, we turn to the nature of mission, that essential quality that applies to any Christian mission and does not change, no matter where the disciple of Jesus finds himself. The text of 2 Corinthians 5 (see the beginning of this chapter) is helpful here, precisely because it doesn't deal with operational details but prefers to call us back to that conscious awareness of God's dreams to which we referred when we were meditating on Moses' call. I invite you, then, to accompany me on a brief exploration of the ministry of reconciliation.

1. The first consideration is that our personal reconciliation with God is the necessary condition for those who would be ministers of reconciliation. Although a person without God is capable of conciliatory and reconciling gestures, the experience of reconciliation with God is fundamental: the person who has not had the experience of knowing that his or her sins and transgressions have been imputed to Jesus is unable to speak correctly about the subject.

By the way, have you noticed how we talk about peace and reconciliation in today's world?

- Reconciliation between nations? – and war machines are constantly at work behind the scenes;
- Reconciliation between people and those who govern them? – it's that social pact for others that no-one wants to keep;
- Reconciliation between humanity and nature? – and we burn everything, throw sewage onto everything and devastate everything;
- Reconciliation between parents and children? – and what we see are 'rich kids', the punks and skin heads, who wreck everything and cover in graffiti everything within reach – monuments, walls, windows… ;
- Reconciliation between husbands and wives? – and fights, coldness and indifference make life a living hell, when they don't end in amicable separation;
- Reconciliation between the flock and the shepherd, the church and her pastor? – and some sheep are autonomous, disagree with the pastor's guidance, think differently, choose another pastor, almost offer to pastor the pastor, and enjoy 'teaching Grandma to suck eggs'.

The one who has not tasted genuine reconciliation, who has not been the target, the object, of the great reconciling act of God's love, is unable to reproduce it properly, fully, in his or her own relationships. Only God's love opens the way for us, teaches us the how of reconciliation and transforms us into reconcilers.

As well as that, we need to think of the intimate heart-reasons behind our participation – or not – in this most noble of all missions. How could a heart full of resentment toward God exercise the mission of reconciliation in an appropriate way? Think of the prophet Jonah. He was sent to Nineveh, but his flight to Tarshish is indicative of his unresolved problems with God. We know the story of what God did in the situation and, once Jonah had completed his mission task among the Ninevites, he waited – in the hope that the promised reconciliation would not happen, that the people would be burned up in a ball of fire.

Poor Jonah! He's mad at God, even claiming that the Most High robbed him of his authority. After all, Jonah had promised, in God's own name, fire from heaven, only to witness a moving reconciliation and national repentance in the end. Because reconciliation was not a part of Jonah's personal experience, it didn't seem either plausible or desirable in Nineveh. It would have been so much easier if God had wiped them out as originally promised.

Jonah raises many issues as we think of the mission of reconciliation. My impression is that this biblical book opens a window on revelation without telling us the whole story. It doesn't tell us what happened before or after the beginning of the Bible narrative and, because of this, we know neither the causes of the prophet's bitterness nor how God completed his reconciling work among the Ninevites. It is with surprise that we observe the Most High holding back patiently and lovingly as he deals with the tiny prophet in an attempt to have a reconciling dialogue with him. I would love to know the outcome of their chat at the end of Jonah Chapter 4.

I draw attention to the fact that this personal experience of reconciliation is possibly what makes all the difference between ministering as one who whose aim is to 'reconcile as he himself has been reconciled', and ministering as Jonah did. How many sons and daughters of pastors and missionaries out there are embittered, feeling their parents treated them like Ninevites! And when God, in his mercy and despite their parents, reaches them and saves them, they face the added sorrow of realising that their parents know very little about joy, that they behave like the elder brother of the prodigal son who was reluctant to go in to the party given by the father for his restored son.

It's possible that this layer of our missionary onion deals with one of the most serious issues in the whole of Christian mission – simply because it touches the heart. I am referring to human affections as well as to the heart of the gospel. It is a layer that speaks of covenant, bread and wine, and without these elements at its very core, there is no Christian mission, either to children or to authorities. It is with pity that I observe many missionaries who are completely burned out. They are good, well-intentioned folk and sincere believers, but struggling to find their space, fighting over ideas, criticising situations (often justifiably), disagreeing with colleagues, spouses, leaders, bosses and so on.

Many of our quarrels and disagreements don't upset us so much, because we didn't start them. We try to be at peace with everyone, but it doesn't depend only on us. In any case, the result is that a life of 'warfare', whether it is waged at home, in the church or at work, undermines our ability to exercise ministry in general. So it doesn't surprise us when a Sunday School teacher feels weak, accused, and without authority to minister the reconciliation that is in Christ to his or her students.

Perhaps one of the trickiest battles that take place in a missionary's heart is that of the pursuit of personal peace. Peace of soul, the peace our Lord bequeathed to his people. Peace only found by thoughtful searching, accompanied by renunciation, dependence on God's provision, and constant prayer. A missionary dedicated to reconciliation can only flourish when their own heart is at peace.

2. The second consideration is that our reconciliation with God produces in us much more than simply the ability to reconcile people by extending to them the blessings we have received. It produces a mission that is continuous, compulsive, permanent and inexhaustible. It is an irrevocable vocation, a call for the whole of life that gives birth to a ministry! Wherever we are, wherever we are sent, whether to *'Stay in Jerusalem'* or to *'Go!'*, or be taken to the ends of the earth by some other means determined by God, we will seek to be a bridge, a way back, a glue that mends what is broken.

If we know that the things that concern our innermost heart are reconciled, then we are 'children of reconciliation' who know how to speak the language of reconciliation: we know its cost, the price paid by Christ, and we know the cross we have to bear; we know that everything comes from God, that the power comes from Christ; and this knowledge makes us into humble ministers. I recall the case of the brother who took a family matter to Jesus hoping for his intervention and for proof of his authority to judge: *Teacher, tell my brother to divide the inheritance with me… Man, who appointed me a judge or an arbiter between you?* (Luke 12:13). Jesus did not come to judge but to reconcile, and it is Jesus' attitude that must become incarnate in our life mission. As far as humanly possible, let's not give up on this ministry.

3. The third consideration that springs to mind is that our mission consists in doing what Jesus did the way he did it. He was the greatest of all ministers. And yet, at some point, we may very well feel some concern about his exercise of this ministry, as we discover that Jesus treated some people harshly, others with mercy. How do we decide what is an appropriate reaction? I have no doubt that Jesus had a better understanding of the human heart than we will ever have. Therefore, unless we receive a specific revelation about a situation, I suggest that we resign ourselves to following the perfect example of the one who did *not count [their sin] against people* (Psalm 32:2). The essence of our mission is to reconcile, to save rather than condemn.

The principal objection to this position comes from the many biblical warnings against false prophets who try to distort the truth and lead astray those brethren whose faith is weaker. While such warnings are indeed plentiful, I suggest we deal with the question in two ways. First, let's not allow ourselves to be contaminated by Jonah's 'righteous' attitude. Of course, cases that arise should be dealt with, but if our attention is always directed to the negative and to the evil in others, that itself can contaminate us, to the point of making us worse than them. Second, let's not judge as individuals but as a group, and by means of mature leaders. When dealing with those who refuse reconciliation and neither hide their wrongdoing nor show any openness to change, repentance or dialogue, the very fact of reacting to the problem as a group dilutes or even removes the emotional component altogether.

On the other hand, the search for incarnation, for being born into the reality, the circumstances, of another is more effective when done at an individual level. In the case mentioned, it might be possible for the leadership to appoint a representative who is emotionally equipped for the task, someone whose own feelings allow him or her to draw close to the other. To take on such a task as an individual rather than in a group setting could easily contaminate the ministry of the 'watchman', even to the point of neutralising any proposed reconciliation.

4. The fourth consideration is that God himself makes available to us a word of power, a word with the power to bring to birth new creatures: *He has committed to us the message of reconciliation* (2 Corinthians 5:19b). Unless we understand this, it's possible that the previous consideration (**3.**) could leave us with a dilemma; we might decide that our mission is after all inglorious or, at the very least, hard to implement. But this verse affirms that the God who made us his ministers by bringing peace to our hearts and reconciling us to himself, also puts into our mouth a power-word that is able to reach right into the soul of a person, into their inmost solitude, into their spirit. And that word can soften hearts of stone.

Notice that verse 19 of 2 Corinthians 5 teaches that *God was in Christ reconciling*; the phrase *in Christ* shows that he is the Word, the Word of God, by whom everything is renewed (v. 17a). And this is the Word that God gave us to administer. Let's go out and administer it then, for we are ambassadors of this Word, *as though God were making his appeal through us* (v. 20). In fact, *as though* is rhetorical, for God literally does speak through us. After the *as though* phrase Paul continues, exhorting: *We implore you on Christ's behalf: Be reconciled to God* (v. 20b).

With that in mind, we return to the Jerusalem mission. It's easy to suppose that a great anointing would be needed for this word to flourish among peoples of pagan cultures, among followers of Eastern religions or even among spiritualists, mystics, sceptics and atheists. But somehow the same anointing doesn't seem so necessary when we are dealing with our children, family, work colleagues, fellow students or even friends at church. Perhaps that is why work on the home front does not challenge us much, and as a consequence, it is not so fruitful. Yes, the enemy does indeed sabotage the missionary factory itself so that it loses its guiding principles and forgets the word at its disposal. God's creative command *Let there be* is silenced and the church ceases to be a living, fasting and praying incarnation of the reconciling Word.

5. The fifth consideration is that the time for reconciliation is *now*. Whether for those to whom we minister or for ourselves, *now* is the time to take up this most honourable, sublime and serious of all challenges. *As God's fellow workers we urge you not to receive God's grace in vain. For he says, 'In the time of my favour I heard you, and in the day of salvation I helped you.' I tell you, now is the time of God's favour, now is the day of salvation* (2 Corinthians 6:1-2).

These words may be read in two equally profitable ways. In the first, the apostle invites *us* to be reconciled. In his letter, Paul strikes a note of urgency, speaking very directly to the Corinthians while at the same time exhorting them as a father. For today's readers, the words come to us with the same urgency and the same exhortation that the reconciling grace of God must not be received in vain. However, what does the text actually mean if the apostle is speaking to believers? My understanding is that Paul considers it impossible to exercise ministry without an experience of reconciliation with God, and is calling us to that faith experience. The second aspect is that the grace of God that must not be received *in vain* is the very ministry God has given us, the ministry of reconciliation. So the apostle is exhorting us not to put that to one side, as though intending to think about it on another occasion.

If the exhortation tells us that *today* is the day of salvation and that the most opportune time is *now*, then we have a duty to think both of ourselves and of those to whom we are sent, those to whom we have been called. As I do that, I am aware of the feeling that urgency grows in inverse proportion to distance. I don't know if I represent the typical evangelical here, but I fear that it's much easier to admit the urgency of reaching the *ends of the earth* than *Jerusalem*. Maybe the daily routine numbs us to the supreme importance of reconciling things at home, at work, in our place of study and in our personal lives, so we just drift on, and let the gentle swaying of the boat rock us to sleep.

If, in any way, this is how we feel, the apostle Paul comes as quite a shock, for he is exhorting us to an immediate change of attitude. *Today* is the time for mission at home, at school, in the church and in the neighbourhood. *Today* is the time to ask ourselves how to do it, what strategies to employ, what help to seek, what preparation is necessary, what should be our goals, and where to seek support in prayer and intercession. To summarise, *today* is the day to fill ourselves to the brim with all those concerns and worries that we can observe in the missionaries we know, for the fact is that we ourselves can wait no longer.

Let's remember Moses' call that we've already discussed, and particularly his sense of complete consternation as he thought about his incompetence for the task entrusted to him. Perhaps he reckoned God had made a mistake in choosing him as a missionary, or that Aaron should have received the call instead. But God had no-one else to send so he asked Moses, *What is that in your hand?* (Exodus 4:2). Then God performed several miracles to show Moses that the mission would be accomplished, not by his personal competence, but by the power of the One who was sending him.

So too for us. If, at this moment in time when we find ourselves face to face with the Apostle Paul's exhortation, we resort to blaming our lack of preparation for our procrastination, we need to remember that maybe God will only ask us for five loaves and two fish. God will multiply whatever we have in our hands as long as we set out in obedience and faith.

Now, setting out on that journey does not mean disagreeing with our children, our spouse, friends – with everybody everywhere. It means setting our heart on the best possible exercise of our ministry; it means being prepared for changes, for conversions, for all the preparation our mission requires; and it means doing all that *now*. And, like a gift from heaven itself, the very 'heart of the onion' will appear in the form of a heart that loves and acts, even when sacrifice is involved. Then things will happen: we will be granted a vision as to how to incarnate our call, a vision of the 'where', of the 'to whom', of the words to be said, the opportunities, the sharing, the being present, the exercise of mercy, the desire to save others.

At this stage in ministry, discernment is vital and this may slow us down, for we may need to divide the task into several steps. But one thing is certain:

now is the moment for genuine heart-acceptance of God's commissioning. Everything else will fall into place at the right moment. But, right from the outset we can begin – for example, by taking steps to get some necessary qualifications. In other words, even when fasting in our secret room, we can be already exercising our ministry.

6. The sixth and final consideration is very down-to-earth. If we are ministers of reconciliation, we will live – yes, in the centre of God's will for our lives; but we will have trials. *Rather, as servants of God, we commend ourselves in every way: in great endurance; in troubles, hardships and distresses; in beatings, imprisonments and riots; in hard work, sleepless nights and hunger; in purity, understanding, patience and kindness; in the Holy Spirit and in sincere love; in truthful speech and in the power of God; with weapons of righteousness in the right hand and in the left; through glory and dishonour, bad report and good report; genuine, yet regarded as impostors; known, yet regarded as unknown; dying, and yet we live on; beaten and yet not killed; sorrowful yet always rejoicing; poor, yet making many rich; having nothing, yet possessing everything* (2 Corinthians 6:4-10).

It's as though Paul has taken an X-ray of his own ministry – as well he might! Of all Christ's apostles, he was probably the one who best understood the meaning of the incarnation of Jesus, and set his heart on imitating him to the point of desiring *to be found in him*. This mindset placed him in a conflict zone, in a field full of dangerous mines set to trap the unwary. That is what incarnation is, the place where the struggle between the spirit and the flesh becomes more acute.

Many trials will challenge and try to discredit our ministry but, if we are new creatures, in the end all of them will *commend* us as God's ministers: Paul presented his sufferings and tribulations as ministerial credentials. We should not be surprised if we face daily trials for, above all else, they will commend us – yes, *us!* – as being genuine ministers of God.

It's worth noting that the conflicts cited by the apostle are not internal, for peace with God is already a reality in his life, even if not yet fully achieved. Of course, there are struggles to be faced, but peace and reconciliation of heart are present spiritual realities that can be shared.

For some time, it never occurred to me that my 'home ministry' could be vested with such dignity, such importance. And here I return to the theme of this book, my emphasis throughout. Let's not deceive ourselves; let's not allow ourselves to be put down by the brilliance of the full-time missionaries we know. Of course, I'm not suggesting any frivolous spiritual pride, but rather an attitude of dignity appropriate to those who also have heard God's call and decided to serve him. I am proposing a new appreciation of our personal ministry in and to 'Jerusalem', for its challenges are as big and as important as those we are accustomed to hearing about from the folk sent abroad as messengers of our church or mission.

6. Easter in Jerusalem

Do you understand what I have done for you? (John 13:12).

We have already thought about the first phase, the first mission field of the one who witnesses to Jesus, as in Acts 1:8. And we noted that Jesus promised the power of the Holy Spirit in order that the mission might be accomplished; and that the birth of Jesus was a sign of the first Christian mission which, when peeled back like an onion, reveals love (the heart of God), incarnation and action. The motive was love, and the action, incarnation.

We then developed the idea that incarnation is a process of identification associated with renunciation; it is permanent renunciation; it is a total lifestyle comparable with a healthy eating plan that ends only when life ends, and which can bring compensations and joys for the participant. Incarnation also speaks of method and attitude, both observable in the example and teaching of Jesus, and therefore prescribed for today's missionaries.

In this chapter, the text we shall look at speaks of one of the last events of Jesus' earthly life, the Passover celebration and the institution of the Lord's Supper. I believe this text contains the secret to Christian happiness – a 'secret' because understanding it is not something revealed to everybody but reserved for those who wish to imitate their Master in his mission of reconciliation. The passage is as follows:

It was just before the Passover Festival. Jesus knew that the time had come for him to leave this world and go to the Father. Having loved his own who were in the world, he loved them to the end.

The evening meal was in progress, and the devil had already prompted Judas, the son of Simon Iscariot, to betray Jesus. Jesus knew that the Father had put all things under his power, and that he had come from God and was returning to God; so he got up from the meal, took off his outer clothing, and wrapped a towel around his waist. After that, he poured water into a basin and began to wash his disciples' feet, drying them with the towel that was wrapped around him.

He came to Simon Peter, who said to him, 'Lord, are you going to wash my feet?' Jesus replied, 'You do not realise now what I am doing, but later you will understand.'

'No,' said Peter, 'you shall never wash my feet.'

Jesus answered, 'Unless I wash you, you have no part with me.'

'Then, Lord,' Simon Peter replied, 'not just my feet but my hands and my head as well!'

Jesus answered, 'Those who have had a bath need only to wash their feet; their whole body is *clean.* And *you are clean, though not every one of you.'* For he *knew who was going to betray him, and that was why he said not every one was clean.*

When he had finished washing their feet, he put on his clothes and returned to his place. 'Do you understand what I have done for you?' he asked them. 'You call me "Teacher" and "Lord", and rightly so, for that is what I am. Now that I, your Lord and Teacher, have washed your feet, you also should wash one another's feet. I have set you an example, that you should do as I have done for you. Very truly, I tell you, no servant is greater than his master, nor is a messenger greater than the one who sent him. Now that you know these things, you will be blessed if you do them' (John 13:1-17).

Although the disciples are unaware of it, these are Jesus' final moments of being physically present with them. The Master already knows that from there they will go to the Mount of Olives, where Judas will betray him. So Jesus gathered his disciples for the celebration of the Passover Supper, one of Israel's most important religious feasts: historically speaking, it was instituted by God as a prophetic enactment of deliverance from Egypt; in spiritual terms, it symbolised Israel's separation from the 'land of bondage', and as such, according to the book of Hebrews, the Passover Supper is an image of the great future that awaits God's people.

Present at the supper is the promised Son, about to fulfil in his own body the ancient promise of deliverance by making a complete and final atonement for our sins. The paschal Lamb will be slain for the last time, a guarantee of eternal salvation, and from now on, there will be no need for any other means of salvation. It will be sufficient to believe in Jesus, to hand over our burdens to him, and submit our soul and will in surrender to his Lordship.

Jesus chose the moment of the Passover meal to teach one last lesson, the most important of all. The prerequisites for the students were that they had been in Jesus' company for three years, that they were his people, and understood the reasoning behind their mission in the world. Without fulfilling these prior conditions, they would not be able to assimilate the content of Jesus' teaching.

What will be the content of this most important lesson of all? The disciples already know that their mission is to go into the world and teach all the things they have already learned. What is lacking then? My understanding is that Jesus will now teach them *how* to do this by giving them, as it were, their inheritance: 'Look at me! Now go out and *do as I have done!* You also must do this for each other in the same way as I, your Master, have done.' So what happens at the Supper is Jesus' last metaphor of his life among the disciples, and his recommendation is that they put *The Parable of Foot-washing* into practice in their ministry life and service.

I hold that, more than a lesson in humility, Jesus was establishing a priestly order, the universal priesthood of foot-washing, to which belong a great multitude of those who, having understood the teaching, seek the power of the Spirit to equip them with all they need to begin serving Jesus in his way. They will become knights performing anonymous acts of service, not-so-secret

'secret agents of the Kingdom', builders of a new and civilising Order, the Order of the 'greater-lesser', the Order of Service.

A first hint as to the possibility of this reading comes from the almost amusing and certainly disconcerting dialogue between Peter and Jesus. Among other things, Jesus said, *Unless I wash you, you have no part with me.* 'Peter, Peter,' says the Master, 'I am establishing my Kingdom, and those who are part of it both wash the feet of others and allow others to wash their feet. If you don't allow me to wash your feet, you are excluding yourself from the spiritual Order I am inaugurating and excluding yourself from the ministry of reconciliation.'

We realise at this point that our distinctions between *mission* and *missions* lose their usefulness. The fact is that we have penetrated so deeply into the 'centre of the onion' that what Jesus teaches and institutes at this time, as part of the sacrament of the Lord's Supper, cannot be divided.

So, as we continue to think about our mission to Jerusalem, I would like to raise three aspects of this solemn passage: the implications of Jesus' teaching, how he acted out that teaching in the company of his disciples, and his closing question: *Do you understand what I have done for you?*

1. In the first place, this dramatic moment tells us that Jesus wanted to teach us to be foot-washing ministers and that this ministry involves saying 'Yes!' to the call to wash the feet of others. If we do not respond by volunteering spontaneously, we will be of no use in the Kingdom.

We have already discussed at some length how the mission of incarnation involves discovering (from God) the identity of those to whom we are sent, and then going to them to evangelise and disciple them, by means of teaching and building them up in the Scriptures. In time, they too will become sufficiently mature to continue in the faith and bear fruit until, as we learn from Jesus' Ascension, we can leave them to go it alone. That is always a difficult moment for parents and children.

Well, here is a clear and direct call from Jesus: *Now that I, your Lord and Teacher, have washed your feet, you also should wash one another's feet. I have set you an example, that you should do as I have done for you* (John 13:14-15). These words both commission us and set up a mission, a calling, to serve one another. Perhaps we can understand this call as a sub-mission, a mission subordinated to the larger one. Note that, at this point, the ministry of reconciliation takes on a new aspect arising from the way it is exercised – namely, by foot-washing, by service. This means that to be a disciple of Jesus is to be a washer of feet in the sense of serving others in the perspective of the Kingdom of God.

Jesus' dialogue with Peter shows that there is no other way to imitate the example of the incarnation as far as our attitude to ministry is concerned, for if we are not willing to serve, we exclude ourselves from the Order of Foot-washing, and therefore the power made available to this Order is no longer at our disposal. We're not the main target audience of the ministry entrusted to us – our neighbour is! Jesus calls us to be God's helpers, in Paul's language, co-workers, ambassadors of the Order and possessing a clear purpose – that of reconciling the world with the Father.

Note that the power of Pentecost as promised in Acts 1:8 is in no way intended to make us happy, prosperous, important, envied, feared or other such inconsequential things. There is a mission to fulfil and Jesus calls us to get involved in it, to co-operate with him in its fulfilment. No matter how obvious it may seem, it is important to emphasise that the foot-washing call was not an end-of-course diploma Jesus wanted to award to his disciples or, by extension, to subsequent generations of followers. Rather, it was a task to be undertaken at the price of their lives, a task not unlike that of a candle: for the candle to give light, it has to be consumed and it receives its reward only when it has burned out, and not before.

2. The second lesson that the supper scene suggests is that, by instituting the Order of Foot-washing, Jesus was also instituting an environment, a culture or way of living the new life that he would bequeath to us through his death on the Cross; this way of life would be the indelible mark of all who accept his invitation to be reconcilers, whether that is made directly, or indirectly through our ministry. Jesus revealed to us his way of living when he decided to shorten the distance between heaven and earth and build his tent among us as God's missionary. This means that the call of Jesus is a call to renounce other ways of living, other ideals regarding life and comfort, other longings and aspirations that may interfere with the task in hand or delay the outworking of the main mission. It also means that the initiates in this Order must make it their exclusive priority. They are ministers of foot-washing first of all, and only afterwards an employee, student, husband, father, elder or whatever. As well as that, some roles in society will be forbidden to them because they are totally incompatible with their main mission, while others will harmonise with it.

Thus, roles and positions whose principal objective entails the exercise of temporal power will be very problematic for the minister, to the point of even distracting him from his prior personal mission and compromising his loyalty to the Order. And I am including politics here, unless it is a self-sacrificing pursuit of the common good. The exercise of power is incompatible with the exercise of love, unless that power is attuned to the mission undertaken, motivated by love (with the sacrifices which that implies) and carried out in the pattern and the spirit of the incarnation. The same applies to other spheres of power, such as the power of parents and spouses, economic power, ecclesiastical power, etc. The fundamental need is to discern the primacy of foot-washing, and failure to do that risks missing our calling and so becoming useless servants, useful neither to the One who called us nor to those to whom we have been sent.

Perhaps the incompatibility between power and love is not so clear. It is worth reflecting that the foot-washing scene serves as a lens used to enlarge a tiny object until it is visible to the naked eye. The fact that Jesus' act shocked Peter is proof that it clearly revealed an inversion of values. He says that Jesus will never wash his feet because he reasons in categories of honour, power and glory, and will not allow his Master to be humiliated; if Peter can avoid it, the Master will not wash his feet. And he thinks that his attitude is honouring to his Lord. In fact, Jesus may have been counting on Peter's reaction to make the point of the lesson clear: the new Order he is inaugurating will be restricted to those who embrace the radical change of values he requires. Love, and not power, rules; and to sacrifice is more important than to be served. The Cross which would be lifted up the next day is the magnificent demonstration of this attitude.

3. There is another lesson to be learned from this disconcerting scene, and because it is counter-cultural, learning this Kingdom value will be painful and many will actually give up on it. Peter's reaction when he said that he would not allow Jesus to wash his feet compelled the Master to tell him: *You do not realise now what I am doing, but later you will understand* (John 13:7). Jesus' teaching here contains a mystery reserved for insiders. Many will not understand it when they observe our best moments (our worst moments will certainly make them comfortable), for such a paradigm shift does not happen immediately, nor painlessly. And that something that applies just as much to us who go as it does to those to whom we are sent.

The activity of the foot-washing minister is to find spaces, motives, excuses and opportunities to serve, and to rejoice when we find them. Even when faced with refusals (13:8a), we attempt to develop deep ties that could lead to serving, for *unless I wash you, you have no part with me*. It is as though foot-washing makes communion possible; foot-washing means serving even when those whom we serve do not yet understand it; foot-washing is to serving even when we ourselves do not yet understand.

I end these thoughts with a look at my Jerusalem. My eyes closed, I see some servant-ministers who are busy, tired, perspiring, and… happy! I would even say that they are fulfilled. To chat to some of them is to discover that they lack nothing and aren't going through some age-related crisis. They aren't stressed by the transition from adolescence to youth, nor from youth to adult life. They don't suffer much at all from mid-life crises nor do they resent old age. Why is that? It is because they do not suffer from an identity crisis; at any age, in any place, they know who they are, even if quite unconsciously. They are God's ministers and in his service. They work constructively in any circumstance and in any environment; they are always busy in their different ways; they are always attentive to needs, always useful. Even in old age, they bear fruit and display luxuriant foliage (Psalm 92:14).

The work is so costly, their love so sacrificial, the adversities so great, the incomprehension so clear for all to see, that there is not much energy left over for personal crises, for doubts born of the emptiness and boredom of the modern world. They always discover another need that demands attention, prayer, inventiveness, creativity, effort, and looking for help.

Then I take another look at my Jerusalem and, with sadness, see people who have lost the vision for foot-washing. People who have begun to seek a cure for their melancholy in films, television, parties, shopping malls, happy hours, business trips, travelling, studies, new jobs, job application processes, etc. Of course, there is nothing intrinsically wrong with these activities, but when they become the main source of our security, emotional comfort, purpose, meaning or identity, they become enemies of the priestly Order of Foot-washing. As I contemplate these people, some very young but looking lost, sad and depressed, I enquire about what they're doing with their lives. The answer I get does not include charitable work with some NGO, a prison evangelisation programme, being on a rota for visits to a hospital, or doing church-based activities. Work (or study) and fun take up most of their time. Normally, such people don't teach in Sunday School, they don't lead anything, they don't participate in any team. They feel lonely and helpless, their lives are in a chaotic state, and that is the root of their sadness.

As always, there are exceptions but, in general, these are people who have not discovered the structuring, guiding, synergistic power of Christian service. They pray little because their needs are few: only their own. They feel no need for the power of the Spirit and don't seek it, because they do not have to deal with anything above what their own strength, persistence and creativity can deal with. They live little, because they live only their own small, boring and restricted lives. They do not understand much about mission to Jerusalem, much less about foot-washing. In fact, as far as these people are concerned, this Order is secret in the negative sense of the word.

To be a missionary in one's Jerusalem is to respond *in a practical way* to the call to foot-washing. I remember a time when I didn't want to sing the song *A New Vessel* because I was afraid of Africa. The song says, *Break my life, and make it anew*, but like Jonah, I didn't want to risk it. However, I discovered that if I did accept the call to Jerusalem, my life would be filled with meaning, because Jerusalem is where my children, friends, parents, wife and co-workers are, and that, automatically, I was being sent to them. Incarnation in love and renunciation was natural and compulsory, and foot-washing would pave my soul with the pursuits, yearnings, struggles and joys of the Kingdom.

Washing one another's feet means humbling oneself and serving practically, effectively, objectively and constructively. When I read Acts 1:8, I hear the following words: 'I will pour out the power of the Holy Spirit in order that Rubem is transformed; so that he has an opportunity to set an example to his children; so that he prays with his children, brothers, friends (thus washing their feet, as it were); so that he goes to church regularly (even when other priorities appear, or when he simply doesn't feel like it) and, by going, teaches them about church attendance, belonging, involvement, and the sufferings involved in life in community. I will pour out my Spirit so that Rubem is a good father, son and brother. He will learn that holiness has to be sought diligently in prayer to my Father, for it comes from him. He is its source, for it is the supernatural power of God.

'Yes, and I will also pour out the power of the Holy Spirit so that that brother over there is a good deacon, elder, pastor, youth leader, teacher of small children, worship leader... If only the young men in the worship group, for example, would humble themselves and seek me, they would receive power from the Holy Spirit to play their instruments as David played his harp; they would receive a double anointing to do the foot-washing task of storing the musical instruments carefully, of fixing the sound cables and putting the microphones back in their boxes. By means of this same power, the young worship leader would realise that he is not the centre of attention, nor does he possess some special energy; he would realise that without me he can do nothing that is useful in My Kingdom.'

As I struggle with these things, I find much comfort in Psalm 90:14-17, where it speaks of God as watching us and giving us his seal of approval. I also see in this passage a promise from God to missionaries to Jerusalem, to the 'Passover servants', God's Passover lambs who reflect the image of his Son. *Satisfy us in the morning with your unfailing love, that we may sing for joy and be glad all our days. Make us glad for as many days as you have afflicted us, for as many years as we have seen trouble. May your deeds be shown to your servants, your splendour to their children* (Psalm 90:14-17).

I want to finish this chapter by telling you about a shy and introverted, yet courageous, lad who, early in life, learned not to expect mercy, forgiveness or help. He despised affection as being 'sissy'. He didn't realise it, but it would have been great if he had been the object of a foot-washing for children led by someone with a call from God and with God's empowering to exercise a *mission to emotions*. He wouldn't have had to wait fifty years to be able to understand his hurts and needs which he, naturally and mistakenly, interpreted as guilt.

When he was small, he always wanted to be treated by a veterinary surgeon – someone who, in his mind, was a very special kind of doctor who could understand even dumb animals. He would dream that one day a very kind adult would appear; he would be dressed in white and have a special stethoscope round his neck. With a deep, searching look, he would get on his knees and calmly look the boy in the eye; with no need for words, he would understand him just as ordinary doctors understand a patient's problem after a quick examination; in fact, he would understand the lad better than he understood himself.

That kind veterinary surgeon would get right into my soul, and his stethoscope would reveal my secrets, thus helping me to understand my own feelings. Just to understand them would be great. Better still if he were to give me a remedy for my heart or a splint for my fractured soul.

7. Mission and Communication

I concluded the previous chapter recalling my childhood dream of being treated by a veterinary surgeon. The doctor of my dreams, one who understands dumb animals unable to articulate what they are feeling, would be an expert in communication. Maybe we could call him a specialist in incarnation, for the incarnation of the Word teaches us about this special type of mission and calls special people to action in Jerusalem. This third element of mission is located just outside the centre of the onion. I call it 'the communication element'.

We learn from the author of the Epistle to the Hebrews that, "In the past God spoke to our ancestors through the prophets at many times and in various ways, but in these last days he has spoken to us by his Son, whom he appointed heir of all things, and through whom also he made the universe" (Hebrews 1:1-2).

The text states that God decided to take extreme measures. I imagine the divine veterinary surgeon bending down from his immeasurably high, totally unattainable, position (we, just like tiny children, look up and cannot even make out his features), kneeling down at our very own level and gazing into our eyes with such sweetness. And we, children in his eyes, just stop and stare. It's not fear, but a mixture of curiosity and reverence, as if we were looking into the eyes of a large, meek lion a foot away. Its power and greatness are such that our tendency is to close our eyes and say: *Woe to me! I am ruined! For I am a man of unclean lips, and I live among a people of unclean lips, and my eyes have seen the King, the Lord Almighty!* (Isaiah 6:5). But that's not how a child would react. The tendency of a normal child would be to overcome fear and run its hand over the lion's mane.

Much progress has been made in studies on the diffusion of innovations, seeking to understand the phenomena of the adoption and rejection of new ideas. This theme is of particular importance to the Christian missionary, whether he or she be a Sunday School teacher, pastor, denominational leader, youth leader, or in any other ministry. Why is that? Because important recent discoveries in this area of communication have come from an unexpected source: Christianity. This means that academics are discovering, albeit reluctantly, what Christians have known (or, at least, they should have known) for two thousand years – namely, that they already have in their midst the greatest example, the perfect paradigm of communication: Jesus Christ, God incarnate.

In the verses quoted, the author of Hebrews teaches us that God communicated with men throughout history in many ways, some of them quite strange. Once he made a mule speak (Numbers 22:28); on another occasion, mysterious fingers wrote on a wall (Daniel 5:5); on yet another, a voice thundered directly from heaven (Matthew 3:17). But we are concerned here with the revelation mentioned in Hebrews 1:2 – namely, that in these last days God has spoken to us through his Son. That is, Jesus was the method made perfect, matured 'in service', complete. *It was fitting that God, for whom and through whom everything exists, should make the Author of their salvation perfect through suffering* (Hebrews 2:10).

How are we to understand this? How can we really see in the incarnate Son of God the prototype of what we ourselves can achieve in terms of communication, a paradigm to be followed? If it were properly developed, would Jesus' understanding of discipleship equip us for a *veterinary-style* ministry? Would we develop that subtle ability to get so close to a soul – which, because of its childish, unconscious reactions and baggage, is burned up by guilt and fear – and enable it to be reconciled with itself, with its neighbour and with God, and find the peace that surpasses all understanding?

In the first chapter of John's Gospel, we find the key verse from which we learn much about God's communication in the light of the above words of Hebrews: *The Word became flesh and made his dwelling among us. We have seen his glory, the glory of the one and only Son, full of grace and truth* (John 1:14). These verses from John and Hebrews suggest at least six lessons on genuine communication that are applicable to all human relationships, particularly to a *veterinary-style missionary* relationship.

The first lesson is simple, for this verse teaches me that communication is much more than words. God had already spoken to his people many times and in many ways through the prophets. He had already used the technique of words. But there came a time when it pleased the Father to make a complete presentation of himself, so that what might be grasped of God was fully manifest to us in his Son. So God stopped talking and went for actions and gestures. He bent down and looked us in the eye. God became incarnate. The Word became flesh and set up his tent (literally *tabernacled,* John 1:14) among us, living alongside us. The very act of incarnation is a clear indication that God wanted to go far beyond the conversations of Old Testament times.

Sadu Sundar Singh, the famous Indian mystic, once walked near an anthill and noticed that the ants fled from his shadow. His first thought was, 'How can I tell them that I won't hurt them?' The answer that came was, 'Only if I could speak their language.' But he soon realised that even that was not enough because, in order to communicate with them, he would need to know their systems, to work out why they were afraid and what kind of threat he posed to them. So he concluded that it was not enough to learn their language. He would have to go further and see life as they did, to see things at their level, to crawl on the ground among leaves, grass and pebbles, to learn how to get into holes, to eat the same vegetation and so on. Even that would not be sufficient: he needed to be accepted by them as one of them, to be seen by them as an ant among ants. Only then would he be able to communicate with them. That was the moment the Sadu understood Christ's meaningful act, his incarnation in all its humiliation and greatness.

To all you wonderful fathers, mothers, teachers and counsellors – you who are called by God to 'Go!' to your local Jerusalem – to you I say that communication is much more than words. It is a silent yet eloquent act, a desire to get close to the point of being 'born' alongside the other. Communication is to do things together, to suffer together. It is to be able to understand a heart that is suffering, confused, trapped, fearful, lost, childlike and, in the end, proud. It is to be able to listen to someone with your *veterinary stethoscope* in your ears and, by the power of God, be received into the *kitchen* of their life. (I will explain about this kitchen in the next lesson.)

The second lesson I take from John 1:14 is that communication requires closeness. The challenge is to move out of the more formal atmosphere of the lounge into the intimacy of the kitchen. God had already spoken from a distance, sending letters (holy books) and people (prophets), but still he was not satisfied. Everything was happening unbearably far away for someone who really loves and wants to save. So, by the gesture of 'dwelling among us', God shortened distance once and for all and became Emmanuel, God near. This drawing nearer of God was complex and includes at least physical and emotional closeness.

With the incarnation, it was immediately possible for God and human beings to walk together along the roads and beaches of Galilee. No longer did he need to shout instructions from above as in Luke 3:22. Now he could take part in people's everyday lives, talk with them about trivial matters, about their work, their family relationships, their dreams and fears, their sins, their hopes. He broke bread with them and taught them about the Bread of Life. He drank wine with them and spoke to their hearts about his new covenant. He looked into their eyes, understood them and was understood by them. Communication requires physical proximity. And, if quality is important, quantity with quality is better still – as much of it as possible, especially as far as children are concerned.

Communion is my word to describe *emotional and affective closeness*. Right from the fall of Adam, God had been seen and understood as powerful, strong, a warrior – but distant, dwelling in the highest heavens and sitting on his sublime throne. Now, incarnate, he shows himself to be a loving Father who is near, who desires contact, warmth and intimacy with his children. And because communication is action, in Luke 15 we find Jesus sitting round the table with tax collectors and sinners and relaxed about being there. His action scandalised the Pharisees who murmured among themselves. 'Too close!' they said. While Pharisees denied that closeness was essential to salvation, Jesus defended it in a memorable series of parables, all on the same theme – the joy of restoration. I refer to the Parables of the Lost Sheep (*Rejoice with me*, Luke 15:6), the Lost Coin (*Rejoice with me*, Luke 15:9) and the Lost Son (*we had to celebrate... the brother of yours... was lost and is found*, Luke 15:32).

Christian missionary, communication requires closeness! A closeness which is much more than physical; emotional and affective closeness; the closeness of someone who takes an interest, who wants the good of another, who wants to know the inner life, the heart, the soul, the problems. A closeness that sits round the kitchen table, goes into that very untidy room, spends time and energy and listens attentively; a closeness that cries with those who cry and rejoices with those who rejoice.

My third lesson is that communication requires a horizontal approach. You will recall what I said about the *ministry of foot-washing*. Jesus' life and words were not about power but about weakness; he did not say things such as, 'Do this because I am telling you to! I'm the leader! I'm the boss!' He did not present his case from a position of power but in a spirit of sacrifice. The great lion looked into our very eyes but did not roar. Had he even shown his fangs – just to make it clear who's who – he would have pushed us so far from him that it would have been difficult to renew dialogue.

The picture of a child fleeing from a lion may be eloquent, but it invites further reflection. There is a childish running away (I mean the child that inhabits us adults) that involves emotions and not legs. Depending on his temperament, a boy can walk away from a bad *veterinary surgeon* without even blinking. He can close himself inside an invisible castle, fasten the powerful locks just as though he were a snail retreating back into its fortress-like shell, and from there nobody will take him out alive.

In Ephesians 5:25 we are taught that any *Head* – that is, leader – should treat those he leads as Christ did the church: *he gave himself up for her*. How many times have I been invited to give an address at a wedding based on this very text – and especially on verses 22 and 23 (*Wives, submit to your husbands as to the Lord. For the husband is the head of the wife*). People forget that the little word *as* appears seven times in verses 22-29. It's a word that compares and sets the standard or model for our leadership: *as to the Lord*. The correct measuring-line is therefore Christ and the church, Christ being the standard for a *husband* and the church the standard for a *wife*. So the recommendation to the husband is: *Husbands, love your wives, just as Christ loved the church and gave himself up for her*. Once again, it is a standard that calls for surrender, humiliation, solidarity and a horizontal approach.

Similarly, the model of authority for governors and public leaders in general, and for their subjection of those who refuse to submit to them which Jesus presented in Matthew 20:25-28, is very different from what we find in secular society: *Not so with you*, he said. *Instead, whoever wants to become great among you must be your servant... just as the Son of Man did not come not to be served, but to serve, and to give his life as a ransom for many*. Christian mission is to get worn out from washing feet. True communication is not done from the top down, from the one who commands to those who obey, from the one who knows to those who don't know, from the one who wields the sceptre of power to the rank-and-file (even though the latter may be treated – condescendingly – as *brothers*). True communication inspires vocations, strengthens the weak, and draws alongside folk with difficulties and limitations. True communication takes place on the horizontal level.

My fourth lesson is that communication is an act of love. We thought about this when discussing peeling the 'mission onion'. At the centre of that 'onion' we discovered a fatherly heart longing for reconciliation and willing to act. As we have already said, love is the starting-point, everything is done in love, every gesture springs from love, and nothing will be accomplished in his Kingdom except by love. Everything is to be poured out in solidarity with the other and by foot-washing; outside this *priestly order* nothing of value can be done, for what is needed is love that washes feet. *For God so loved the world that he gave his one and only Son, that whoever believes in him shall not perish but have eternal life* (John 3:16).

These words affirm that love – and only love – was what motivated the incarnation: *For God so loved the world that he gave.* Not a love of empty words or platonic feelings, but a love that *gave* – and more than that: a love that gave *itself.* That word *itself* is very important in this context, because it is often the case that we are willing to give something in order to avoid giving ourselves. This is very common among fathers, mothers and leaders. We give things to our children to keep them from demanding our presence, our stooping down to their level, our giving of ourselves. But Jesus' love was not like that. It manifested itself with such dramatic intensity that, instead of giving something to us, it *gave itself.*

This is God's gesture of love as revealed in the incarnation of Jesus: it is a love that seeks **reconciliation** (*God was reconciling the world to himself in Christ,* 2 Corinthians 5:19); a love poured out in **solidarity** with others (not seeking its own interests, and weeping with those who weep); a love which becomes **identification** (by assuming our identity, Jesus emptied himself of his glory and humbled himself, taking the form of a servant, even becoming *obedient to death* (Philippians 2:7). Generally, identification is synonymous with renunciation, and renunciation takes on a material dimension in incarnation, as we 'pitch our tent' among those with whom we want to share common ground. I shan't labour this point here for it is the guiding theme of this book, a fundamental presupposition of Christian mission.

To you, my missionary brother and sister in Christ, I say that communication is a gesture, an attitude, a concrete action; it is the fulfilment of a promise; it is the realisation of hope. In communicating, you identify with the people you are evangelising; you get to know what they are thinking and feeling, and that with deep empathy and sacrificial compassion. Perfect communication is a gesture of love.

The fifth lesson we learn from John 1:14 is that communication is a way of serving – back to the 'priestly Order of Foot-washing' that we looked at in the previous chapter.

The prophet Daniel (7:14) foretold that the coming One would be strong and powerful, and was destined to be served by the nations of the earth. Who could have imagined that Christ would come in the way Isaiah 53 describes? Yet, in Luke 9:48, we find Jesus teaching that his way exemplifies simple unpretentious service. *Whoever welcomes this little child in my name welcomes me; and whoever welcomes me, welcomes the one who sent me. For it is the one who is least among you all who is the greatest.* To follow the way of Jesus is to choose death and not life, in the sense that we put others' interests before our own.

To return to the 'onion' of Christian mission, we could say that service is synonymous with renunciation, and that incarnation is identification associated with renunciation. It is a living death but one which finds life by dying. Maybe that's why Jesus taught us that *whoever wants to save his life will lose it, but whoever loses his life for me and for the gospel will save it* (Mark 8:35). The one who, like Jesus, is willing to give up their life, their interests, their comforts, rights and privileges in service to the cause of Christ, will find true life.

To choose the path of service is to choose the Way of the Cross in everyday life. To choose constant self-giving is the most effective way to serve, for serving implies not being distracted by promises of short cuts, easy options or more power – all such deceptive paths. Faced with a choice of personal glory or of service that would lead to a perfect 'mission accomplished', Jesus always chose the latter, even when that route pointed to Jerusalem and the Cross that awaiting him there.

My dear *missionary to Jerusalem*, communication is more than words, more than closeness; more than a stooping down to the other's level; even more than a gesture of love. Communication is **the** way to serve. Without 'foot-washing' we are not sharing with Jesus in his ministry. The one who has not learned to have their feet washed by Jesus and to wash the feet of fellow human beings does not belong to the 'priestly Order of Foot-washing'; they do not understand about pitching a tent, about incarnation, about the *Word* that is light which restores, redeems and reconciles; they do not understand communication.

Finally, the sixth lesson that the incarnation of Jesus teaches is that communication is a continuous crossing of frontiers, of breaking down barriers. The first great act of God's love was consummated when the divide between the divine and the human was crossed. When God became man, the infinite distance, the frontier between natures, dimensions, worldviews and conceptions of life and the cosmos – all was overcome. The incarnation means that God made himself a citizen of the world, becoming God among us, God-man.

But even crossing that frontier wasn't everything, for there were other barriers to be overcome, perhaps even more important than the first because they involved the ransom of those who didn't want to be ransomed. The incarnation by itself would be insufficient to conquer a rebellious, arrogant heart. By getting down on his knees, the veterinary surgeon of my childhood dreams would have seen hard, steely eyes; impenetrable eyes; eyes as rebellious as they were needy; as proud as they were despairing; and as needy as they were incapable of admitting it. Eyes that would hide away in the nearby woods at the time of the campfire altar-call (see Chapter 1); eyes that would become indignant with the failures and weaknesses of the veterinary surgeon; eyes that would rather be defeated than persuaded, but which would never surrender even when conquered by brute force.

Faced with such a situation, Jesus crossed the barriers of distrust, resentment and enmity. As a man, he turned to the Father and said, *Your will be done,* and proceeded to plead that the Father might reign in our hearts. As a man among men, he visited Samaria, a region divided by ancient and deep-rooted enmities and much bitterness, and broke down those barriers, making reconciliation with the Father possible. Jesus was born in Nazareth in 'Galilee of the Gentiles', thus breaking down barriers of poverty, discrimination and prejudice. He became one of them, one of us. And we saw his glory.

Christian missionary, communication is being able to be born into the everyday situation of those you are leading, in order to become one with them, to understand their situation, to suffer their humiliation, to break down barriers that would otherwise be impossible to cross. I once heard a fellow Christian say that he did not like talking to the poor. One thing is certain: he had not yet understood anything of communication by incarnation; he had not yet understood Jesus' act of love; he still did not realise that true communication only occurs by a continuous and tireless crossing of boundaries, of frontiers.

What frontiers are there in Jerusalem? I think of the divide between my middle-class world and the world of poverty. To cross this frontier in order to 'be born' into this other world would be a sacrificial act, but there is no doubt that the result would be a new experience of communion for both parties, perhaps even – if God permits – with redemptive results for all concerned.

I think of the frontiers created by pain and suffering. To be born into a world of grief, loss, sickness, anguish, loneliness, abandonment and abuse, demands preparation and divine anointing, ability and prayer. But it is a way that is guaranteed to make God's love become real to a heart covered by the murky, chaotic waters of pain; to offer them a 'let there be light'; to minister to them something of the regenerating power of him who is the light of men.

There is also the boundary of bitterness and resentment, as was the case of the Samaritans and perhaps of embittered people we ourselves know. To be born into this world demands that the gift of mercy be exercised close-up and with affection and patience. Sometimes, that mercy must be associated with some exhortation and a decision to accompany the other on their long walk back to 'thanksgiving' (because a bitter heart neither worships nor gives thanks, even though it often gives an impression of security and haughtiness). A bitter heart has lost sight of its Lord.

As for the boundary of indifference, in this state of soul, the things of God no longer cause emotion or any other reaction; so to allow oneself to be born into this world requires patience and skill; it requires much time spent knocking at the door and much discernment to detect distress calls disguised as 'Leave me alone!' When an indifferent person eventually opens the door, there will be a banquet of fellowship and salvation.

How many more boundaries are there? They are as numerous as human beings' capabilities of closing in on themselves and of getting lost in labyrinths. And to think that such boundaries make those who are so close to us become so distant! They are within our physical reach, but for some reason unreachable. They have become resistant to communication both of reason and of the gospel. Perhaps the finer form of communication that we learn from the incarnation of the Word is the only hope for them.

True communication, being more than words, shows itself to be a sacrificial love capable of continuous and dynamic togetherness. It desires unity so that two or more become one. It longs to re-create reality, its meanings, values, aims and aspirations, through dramatisations of intense, mature love.

Therefore, if in a missionary project, whether at the ends of the earth or in Jerusalem, there is no genuine communication, then the divine model as seen in Jesus is compromised. The world that prefers to communicate painlessly and at a distance will end up without God's *Word,* and communication will continue to be what we learn from our human teachers. After all, reconciliation is not what they want; they aim to persuade, to sell.

8. For Their Sake – Holiness And Mission

For them I sanctify myself, that they too may be truly sanctified (John 17:19).

This brief reflection on holiness as another aspect of our motivation for mission builds on themes already examined in this book. When dealing with the biblical roots of Christian mission, we spoke about the 'heart of the onion', about visiting the 'missionary factory'. And we emphasised that the voluntary, sacrificial incarnation of the Son – whom the apostle John introduces to us as *the Word of God* – originated in the love of a Father who could wait no longer to act.

We then showed that it is impossible to conceive of a more concrete manifestation of this love than the appearance of the baby boy in the manger. And we concluded that these two aspects, the Father's love and the Son's incarnation, form both the affective presuppositions and the dynamics of any missionary activity arising from a call to the ministry of reconciliation.

Thirty-three years later and the boy is now an adult, doing the work entrusted to him by the Father – and, according to John's Gospel, speaking about holiness and praying for it. He asks the Father to sanctify his disciples and he inclines his own heart to holiness for their benefit.

Our understanding of the need for sanctification, and the pursuit of those personal transformations that accompany our search, normally take place as we pray in the secret place. While holiness must contain a relational element, our search for it is (usually) a very private matter, a solitary, intimate quest that takes place behind closed doors – and Jesus did recommend: *Go into your room, close the door and pray* (Matthew 6:6). It seems that the process is as follows: we ask God, as it were, to strip from us our old self, and we do that for love of God and of our fellow men. However, our chief motivation is our love for God.

The apostle John teaches us that whoever says he loves God must also love his brother (1 John 4:21). When we realise that Jesus was saying these things in prayer and at a time of great personal crisis, we begin to understand that sanctification takes on the character of a sacrificial offering – and in Jesus' case, the purification of the offering of his life in death.

Holiness also has the connotation of separation, of personal consecration – a decision to go after what is right, good, noble and true, and to abandon lying, error, what is false, sinful and of the world. Generally, our motivations are gratitude, love for God, the desire to be happy (*blessed*), and to lay up treasure in heaven – that is, to invest in the invisible.

While all these elements are correct, biblical and desirable, Jesus' all-pervading missionary perspective lays bare a subtle reversal of the polarity that these motives suggest. This becomes clear in his memorable priestly prayer – his final reporting back to the Father – as recorded in John 17. There he says to his Father that a deliberate part of his motivation to holiness is the effect such holiness would have on the disciples. He says he sanctifies himself *for their sake*. This represents a new perspective on Jesus' purpose – 'for them' – and an unexpected source of motivation – 'those whom you gave me'. I imagine hearing him say to his Father, 'I'm not doing this for myself but for those around me, even for those who are yet to be born.' His main motivation is social – it's 'they', the folk who are praying with him in that moment of pain, and folk who are not yet in the church, not yet born – future generations. In order to make this clearer, I propose the following paraphrase: 'I become better (from God's point of view) so that they too may be better. I adjust to the purposes you, God, have determined for my time here, in order that they too may benefit from your purposes for their lives'.

Now for another proposal based on my paraphrase – I suggest that you, reader, try to imagine some personal, practical applications of Jesus' words. Here are some suggestions to get you started:

- In my home, I will avoid the short cuts which come from small lies so that my family may be made perfect in the practice of truth:
    - learning to speak the truth – always;
    - learning to trust what others say without the wearisome need for empty promises;
    - learning about the dignity there is in a simple 'yes' or 'no', as well as about the mercy necessary to live the truth, so that the latter does not become a judge without a soul and a cruel tormentor;
    - learning about the abysses created by the many aspects of lying (falsehood, deceit, setting traps for others, cover-up, a lying silence, vanity, greed, pride and so on).
- I will avoid tobacco products and any signs of drunkenness at home and at parties, whether with family or friends, so that my children do not grow up with the impression that these things are innocent, everyday occurrences, a normal expression of joy and celebration;
- I will avoid licentious language, full of double meanings and erotic, spicy, sensual or openly immoral allusions, so that my children do not grow up thinking that such language is 'normal' – for that is how the world sees it. So I will not encourage such jokes; I will not forward them by email; I will avoid filthy conversations which do indeed corrupt good manners; I will not dress provocatively (we all know the difference between being sensual or lascivious in dress and being attractive); I will not use sensuality and irreverence as a way of sinning in order to become acceptable to my non-Christian colleagues.
- When I need to borrow something, I will return it quickly;
- I will not threaten to do something and then not do it (better not to threaten at all).

An uncomfortable thought comes to mind: if I do all this, I will become a goody-goody, backward-looking and legalistic – just like the Pharisees with their 'You must nots'. That is not my intention. I am not suggesting a return to the self-righteous behaviour of the Pharisees. What I do have in mind is that, alongside that holiness that comes into us *from* the outside, another holiness must flow from us, this time from within us *to* the outside. A holiness born of a desire to bless, in the foot-washing manner, for that is in perfect harmony with 'mission in Jerusalem': *For them I sanctify myself.*

You don't have to follow all the examples I gave, for they are nothing more than examples. Just because it is so limited, the list may not even be useful. However, we can make use of the idea – of Christ's lesson. If we are seeking to grow and mature in the faith, let's also include the missionary dimension in our quest. May the intimate thoughts of our souls and the purest yearnings of our hearts flourish in the garden of mission, there to be irrigated by the altruistic realisation that no-one is even seeing what we are doing and thinking. Perhaps one way to avoid legalism would be to cultivate these things in one's own heart without necessarily imposing them on others, not even on those nearest to us. As the hymn says, *May the beauty of Jesus be seen in me* – and that by God's grace.

A final word of clarification. That phrase *I sanctify myself* does not mean autonomy in relation to God. Jesus would never have admitted such an idea. The best way to understand Jesus' attitude is to see it as an intimate promise he shared with the Father, as if saying, 'Father, I am seeking these higher things in you alone, and for this I depend on the supernatural power of Pentecost. However, if I am seeking them in you alone, I am also doing it for the sake of those you love and have entrusted to me.'

9. The Knowledge of God

In the previous chapter, we looked at Jesus' High Priestly Prayer, his final reporting back to the Father before the conclusion of his mission. Only one – painful – task, the crucifixion, lies ahead. After that, he will return to the Father. We now examine that report in a little more detail, for it helps us to understand our mission, since ours is derived from his and we are his disciples and followers.

> Now this is eternal life: that they know you, the only true God, and Jesus Christ, whom you have sent (John 17:3).
>
> Now they know that everything you have given me comes from you (v. 7).
>
> For I gave them the words you gave me and they accepted them. They knew with certainty that I came from you, and they believed that you sent me (v. 8).
>
> Righteous Father, though the world does not know you, I know you, and they know that you have sent me (v. 25).
>
> I have made you known to them, and will continue to make you known in order that the love you have for me may be in them and that I myself may be in them (v. 26).

I imagine the Beloved Disciple looking over his memoirs as he writes his epistle, certain in his spirit that the genuine love he is proposing for fellow believers is an essential part of the Christian life. In the context, 'genuine' refers to the perfect integration of the vertical and horizontal dimensions of faith. Neither must exist alone; neither, on its own, can give life. The vertical axis points to God, refers to relationship with God. The horizontal axis points sideways, to our neighbour, to fellow Christians. It does indeed seem that it is both wise and coherent to allow one to reveal the other, to help the other, so that it's easy to see that the horizontal dimension without the vertical is as empty as spirituality without works.

Curiously enough, John presents us with the symbol of the Cross, the place where the two axes meet: the stake pointing to heaven, the crossbeam to human beings, to our neighbour. On that Cross, Jesus died and completed his redemptive and reconciling mission. Perhaps that explains why John seeks his model for understanding true spirituality and true mission in the Cross. And so, as he looked over his memoirs, he recalled Jesus' words in his High Priestly Prayer, words he had memorised and written down. And he would have remembered that, in that moment of crisis, Jesus repeatedly mentioned the *knowledge of God*, a subject discussed with the disciples, including John; he had heard the Master say that eternal life is *[to] know you, the only true God* (John 17:3). That was why Jesus had taken care to make sure that his followers knew the only true God, for only thus would they be able to have communion with each other.

Many years had passed before John sat down to write his first letter that arose out of concern that the faith passed on to future generations be genuine: that was John's life mission, carried out in obedience to Jesus who had sent him. There is no doubt that his letters went hand-in-hand with his preaching and teaching, his writing confirming and strengthening his preaching. And as we read what has come down to us, we realise that he was passing on to his fellow Christians and disciples what he had learned at the feet of his Master: a living example of genuine faith which combined devotion to the Father with horizontal love of others, a model of sound spirituality.

I am convinced that the apostle John's teaching has some precious lessons that can guide our missionary activity, whether in Jerusalem, or Judea and Samaria, or to the ends of the earth. They will be useful to those who serve in any aspect of mission anywhere – simply because they bring us back to 'the heart of the onion'. In Chapter 17, John's goal is practical and twofold: the various occurrences of the word 'know' (vs. 7, 8, 23, 26) show that he is seeking both to encourage a greater nearness to God and to provide criteria for discerning the quality of our spiritual life.

The following brief meditation takes as its starting-point the conversation between Jesus and Thomas as recorded in John 14:5; our goal is to examine the text from the perspective of mission. In his final message to the disciples, Jesus declared himself to be the only way to the Father (vs. 6, 7). But Philip insisted, *Show us the Father and that will be enough for us* (v. 8). In fact, Philip was simply following Thomas, who said *Lord, we don't know where you are going, so how can we know the way?* (v. 5)

I don't know about you, but my inclination is to look down on this disciple – just a little. It seems that Thomas never fully understood Jesus' lofty purposes, as though his call to discipleship had been a mistake. And his words here reinforce my impression. However, his very practical words do help to clarify things; for the way ahead always depends on the final destiny, just as the means depend on the end, and the tools used depend on the work to be accomplished. In the same way, the means of mission depend on the work to be done. How can anyone properly fulfil their mission if the nature of mission and its goals are not fully understood? How can anyone know the way without knowing where the Master is going?

Jesus had just said that he would return to the Father and that, while waiting for them to arrive and be with him, he would *prepare a place for them*; he also stated that they knew the way there (v.4). Thomas, bewildered, said, *No, we don't know*. Jesus' reply clarifies the issue, for he insisted that his task on earth was to reveal God, to lead people to a desire to be with God and to live with him in their eternal home (Psalm 23:6). To my mind, that is a summary of the mission of the incarnate Christ: to reveal the Father by revealing himself as the Father's messenger, so that, by knowing him, his disciples might know the invisible Father. The apostle John, speaking of Jesus' mission of revealing and unveiling the Father, uses the language of glorifying God on earth and consummating the work entrusted to him: *Now this is eternal life: that they may know you, the only true God, and Jesus Christ, whom you have sent. I have brought you glory on earth by completing the work you gave me to do* (John 17:3-4).

The text raises an obscure point, but one which is the key to our understanding here. It can be summarised in the question, 'How can God be *known*?' The follow-up question, 'How can we *glorify* God in the world?' is directly linked with Christian mission, for in mission our concern is to do the work entrusted to us and take the message of eternal life to our relatives and friends. After all, **we** know that *this is eternal life: that they may know you, the only true God, and Jesus Christ, whom you have sent.*

So, trusting that I have convinced you that the glorification of God has a missionary dimension, that the task entrusted to us has an effective strategy (as our Master's example clearly showed) and that our paths must be similar to those taken by Jesus – I would like to be so bold as to outline some ideas as to how we could draw this emphasis on the knowledge of God into the scope of *mission to Jerusalem*. I base my thoughts on John's first epistle.

In the first place, John teaches that God can be known through the love we have for each other. Somehow that doesn't sound quite right: shouldn't it be through the love we have for him? The fact is that 1 John 4:7, 11, 20 emphasise the horizontal dimension. Even when writing about loving God in verse 20, John stresses the horizontal, and the same is true of verse 19, a verse frequently interpreted incorrectly; the original is, literally, *we love because he first loved us*. It is not *we love him because he first loved us*. What is this love like? Here John becomes practical, writing *This is how God showed his love... he sent his one and only Son* (v. 9); before we could love him, he sent his Son (v. 10) *that we might live through him* (v. 9).

These two verses remind me of the well-known illustration of footprints in the sand. We walk along leaving footprints as of a child in the sand; suddenly adult footprints appear next to ours, firmer and more powerful; then our tiny footprints disappear, covered over by the larger, deeper footprints of one who is well able to carry an extra weight, to carry us. *This is how God showed his love among us: He sent his one and only Son into the world that we might live through him. This is love: not that we loved God, but that he loved us and sent his Son as an atoning sacrifice for our sins* (1 John 4:9-10).

The second thought, derived from this, is that our love reveals God himself to us and to the world. A careful examination of 1 John 4:12 would suggest a break in the argument, for we might expect that the logical follow-on to *No-one has ever seen God* would be the realisation that there is, in fact, a way to *see* God. What is it? *If we love one another* God becomes visible in us – because God is love. He becomes discernible and comprehensible first to us, then to others.

In Jesus' prayer, referred to earlier, he gave his report to his Father, saying that he had revealed God. I want to stress the words *that the world may know* (John 17:23). More than that: our practice of genuine love will not only make God known to us and the world, but also to the rulers and authorities in the heavenly realms: *that now, through the church, the manifold wisdom of God should be made known to the rulers and authorities in the heavenly realms, according to his eternal purpose which he accomplished in Christ Jesus our Lord* (Ephesians 3:10-11).

Thirdly, John suggests to us that God can be known from the fact that the Spirit given us by God is a Spirit of love. It's common to recognise some traits of parents in their offspring and say, 'You are just like your father' – and we are referring not only to their physical appearance. In the same sense, the Holy Spirit helps us to love, shows us what love is, and leads us as we practise it. *This is how we know that we live in him and he in us: he has given us of his Spirit* (1 John 4:13). In what sense does the Spirit enable us to know God better? It seems to me that baptism in the Spirit makes us children of love – *born of God* (v. 7) – and is the means by which God pours out his love into our hearts (Romans 5:5) and leads us to practise love.

We may conclude by saying that this amazing epistle of John teaches that knowing God is intimately related to the mission of loving as he loved (v. 11), and to make us perfect in the 'how' of loving as described in verses 9 and 10. On the other hand, we know that these things are being made perfect in us when we perceive his Spirit in us (v. 13; Romans 5:5). The key to our love is his love (v. 19). How do you, my reader, answer the question of v.20: 'Do you know God?' If you are able to answer affirmatively, you will also know that you are God's minister, commissioned to glorify him. And that mission will fill up every space of your life.

Another consequence of knowing God is that we no longer fear the Day of Judgement, because we will be like him. *This is how love is made complete among us so that we will have confidence on the Day of Judgement: in this world we are like him* (1 John 4:17). *Perfect love drives out fear* (v. 18).

Are we longing to get to know God better? We need to look upwards, but also sideways. Yes, that is my understanding of the essence of mission: *Everyone who loves has been born of God and knows God* (v. 7). Love your neighbour and you will learn a lot about God. Love your neighbour and you will be carrying out the work entrusted to you. The end-point of this great story of love will be just as the prophet Habakkuk foretold: *For the earth will be filled with the knowledge of the glory of the Lord, as the waters cover the sea* (Habakkuk 2:14).

10. Mission Strategies

I bring this book to an end looking at some consequences of the reflections presented, beginning with strategies. Strategies are deliberate plans as to the ways and means of doing things efficiently. Missionary strategy also involves this type of planning but in close association with prayer, and for this reason a missionary strategy will mature in the heart when presented to God in prayer, and with diligence and humility.

Efficiency is the strategists' key word for they are always dealing with a lack of resources and therefore must know both the resources they have and the best way to use them. Hence the quest for efficiency, which we may think of as the way to achieve *the best result at the lowest cost*. At the very least, planning involves:

- Knowledge of the environment (whether favourable or unfavourable) in which the task will be performed;
- Knowledge of the techniques and processes involved;
- Knowledge of both the conditions and the limitations of actions to be taken (whether in relation to physical, financial or human resources), including competencies and lack of the same;
- Visualising of possible scenarios to avoid surprises;
- Planning round issues of key control points and default mechanisms;
- Deciding on a 'Plan B'.

Missionary strategies seek to optimise the use of financial and human resources with a view to doing missionary work among a specific race, people, nation, group, city, neighbourhood, clan, family or individual.

Our argument throughout this book has been that some strategists assume that, as far as Christian mission is concerned, Jerusalem is well served precisely because it is 'the factory'. For that very reason, few have a missionary strategy for Jerusalem, preferring – quite rightly – to leave the task to the local church.

On the other hand, when thinking strategically about missions, the local church usually focuses on sending missionaries to 'the ends of the earth'. Therein lies the problem. We imagine that because we live in Jerusalem, the missionary factory, we are living among missionaries. That ought to be true. However, at the same time, we display the parallel mentality of 'Go to some distant place!' The net result is confusion: if our missionaries are not distant from us, it's because they're not where they should be. So, at one and the same time, we live in 'the factory', but we do not live among missionaries, because we do not live as missionaries. We only see the 'real missionaries' when they have reason to visit the missionary base. And their reporting back makes us feel humiliated.

However, if this perception of Jerusalem as forgotten from the point of view of missionary strategy is true, it is not difficult to explain why 'the factory' will gradually become less efficient (quantitatively and qualitatively) as a 'producer' of missionaries. I can't say if our church is typical, but I personally do not know any missionary who is a son or daughter of long-standing members of our church. Normally, our church's missionaries are either missionary kids or young people from outside the church who have been 'adopted' by us; folk converted somewhere else and, who by God's mysterious ways, came to us. However, the expression 'missionary kids' itself suggests some degree of exclusion; children of missionaries who accept the missionary call should be our children – *all* of them.

With this in mind, and based on the motivation and the method undergirding Christian mission, as well as on an understanding of the necessity and urgency of the church's involvement with intro- mission, I now present some strategic ideas for 'Jerusalem'. My list is in no way exhaustive, but it is fruit of my involvement in my own 'Jerusalem world'. This world (which may not be the same as yours) encompasses the following social roles: father, mother, son, daughter, teacher, worker, husband, wife, boyfriend, girlfriend, other church members, deacon, elder, church missionary.

The first change I would like to see is the church in Brazil totally saturated with the missionary spirit. I can easily imagine that this phrase will offend the army of men and women of God whose ministry is already dedicated to missions. But if you have read what we've talked about so far, you will know that I'm not speaking of these folk. On the contrary, I thank God for these selfless brothers and sisters. What I am saying is that my dream is for the whole church to be impregnated with the spirit of intro-mission, with simply getting involved everywhere and in everything. You will recall that, earlier in the book, I use 'intro-mission' as a metaphor for concern about the Jerusalem dimension of missionary work.

So you want to discover who it is you're sent to? Great! The starting-point is to recognise that everyone has been given some task in the great reconciling mission of Christ: *he gave us the ministry of reconciliation*. To become impregnated with the spirit of intro-mission, as I use that word in this book, is to realise that we are all commissioned by God. We are missionaries wherever we are. We need to know that we have already been sent to our children, parents, spouses, friends, colleagues, local church – no-one is outside the Jerusalem project unless he or she has been sent to Judea, Samaria or to the ends of the earth. And, in fact, if such a missionary has their family with them, they too have their own little Jerusalem to care for. The idea that 'I haven't been called to any mission at all' is a trap set to prevent us from noticing the sad phenomenon of the branch separated from the vine. Perhaps this is a good time to look at mission to those near us from the perspective of the vine:

I am the true vine, and my Father is the gardener. He cuts off every branch in me that bears no fruit, while every branch that does bear fruit he prunes so that it will be even more fruitful. You are already clean because of the word I have spoken to you. Remain in me, as I also remain in you. No branch can bear fruit by itself; it must remain in the vine. Neither can you bear fruit unless you remain in me.

I am the vine; you are the branches. If you remain in me and I in you, you will bear much fruit; apart from me, you can do nothing. If you do not remain in me, you are like a branch that is thrown away and withers; such branches are picked up, thrown into the fire and burned (John 15:1-6).

In my opinion, these words of Jesus are positive, stimulating and comforting, and not merely intended to cause fear, as so many seem to think. Before I take a good look at the branch being cut down and thrown into the fire because it bears no fruit, I take time to absorb the joyful news that, in the end, the mission of each one of us is to bear fruit. I reckon that much of our anguish, far from disqualifying us, is caused by the farmer's pruning our branches so that we can produce even more fruit. Furthermore, I believe that it is only after we realise that Jesus is speaking of missions that we face the challenge to examine our life: 'Come and believe, either out of fear or out of joy, that *If you remain in me and I in you, you will bear much fruit.*' However, the one who remains in him but bears no fruit is cut off.

The way mission is worked out in the personal life of each Christian is so varied that I would not dare to describe it. But it is important to fight against the idea that mission to the family or local church – that is, to the inside – is a lesser or less demanding mission from the standpoint of Kingdom strategies. Maybe what's missing is just this local sending. Yes, it does seem a paradox: as we have already stressed, we are usually concerned with sending missionaries to faraway places. However, strategic thinking leads me to propose that churches marked by the missionary spirit develop a conscious programme for sending missionaries to their local area. I believe that such a formal, explicit, public and community gesture is capable of strengthening missionary awareness among many fathers, mothers, children, workers, students and so on – all people of 'Jerusalem'.

To pursue my argument here, I call your attention to a Pauline text widely used in messages about mission to faraway places: *How can they preach unless they are sent?* (Romans 10:15). I would go further and propose that we adopt the whole of Romans 10:1-20 as our 'motivational and programmatic content' for mission to those near at hand. So how would it be if we we if we were to read verses 13 to 15 as though the apostle Paul was discussing intro-mission with members of our local church? Imagine him talking to the pastor about the need to make sure that mothers and fathers are clear about their mission to their children. His words hit hard: *Everyone who calls on the name of the Lord will be saved. How, then, can they call on the one they have not believed in? And how can they believe in the one of whom they have not heard? And how can they hear without someone preaching to them? And how can anyone preach unless they are sent? As it is written, 'How beautiful are the feet of those who bring good news!'* (Romans 10:13-15).

As I look at this passage again, I cannot avoid reviewing my own Christian journey and noticing there – and in the lives of many fellow travellers – an absence of any awareness that we have been sent to our children. Yes, 'Sent', and that with all the solemnity attached to the priesthood of all believers. I further conclude that we are totally unaware of this sending because of a failure in the church; there is no systematic programme surrounding the act of sending, with an appropriate liturgy that is celebrated repeatedly and in many different ways, as local tradition requires. Judging by my own experience, people find it difficult to absorb the concept of a formal sending ceremony focussed on home mission, whether to the neighbourhood or to the workplace. Of course, they know that the Christian life ought to be a constant life of witness, but they do not always see it as a life of mission.

To a certain extent, verse 2 supplies me with mitigating factors that support my argument: *They are zealous for God, but their zeal is not based on knowledge*. In fact, for a long time I had no conception at all of the importance of simply confessing my faith in the family: *If you declare with your mouth, 'Jesus is Lord', and believe in your heart that God raised him from the dead, you will be saved. For it is with your heart that you believe and are justified, and it is with your mouth that you profess your faith and are saved* (Romans 10:9-10).

I want to confess to you, my reader, how many times I have missed the chance to prophesy what God was about to do before anything happened, and so an event would go unnoticed by my family because of my silence. God did act mightily – as I knew he would – but the miracle was not noticed nor its Author glorified, because of the timid silence of a missionary with no awareness of intro-mission. To say, as many like to do, after the blessing has been granted, 'I knew it would all work out!' does nothing to mend matters.

Churches ought to encourage their members, individually or in groups, to 'Go!' to those to whom they are sent, especially to their children, spouses, friends, work colleagues, to other believers and even to the local church itself. And to develop teaching about evangelism, witness, the exercise of the priesthood of all believers at any time and in any place – or rather, with no need for particular times or spaces – and with all wisdom.

If love is what motivates incarnation, may we all be encouraged to seek God **in order to** fulfil this mission, both collectively and individually. Such a proposal may not seem very strategic. The fact is that the stimulus to seek God cannot be left out of any aspect of Christian discipleship. I mention it here, in this missionary context, to show the strategic character of what we are proposing. Another 'take', as it were, on seeking the qualifications for a witness born of love.

Behind this insight is the understanding that we cannot act as a branch detached from the vine. The awareness of mission that is born when your child is born, when you get married, matriculate in a school, or take on a responsible job, requires corresponding spiritual resources. These resources must be sought diligently, for they are the indispensable means to the fulfilment of the *mission*, just as much as they are (or ought to be) in the case of a trans-cultural missionary. Furthermore, this mission will be clearly identified by the local church and the missionary will be symbolically, liturgically and formally 'sent out'.

Through this way of being a local church, the young man who gets his first job will be the object of the missionary attention of the church (I want to avoid the idea of a department, a little box on an organisational chart), and will immediately receive preparation, a vision as to his potential ministry, specific training, prayer – and a formal, public and liturgical sending out in the name of Jesus.

Similarly, a couple will look on their baby as the first priority of their ministry of reconciliation. And they will seek in God the strength, discipline, knowledge of the 'task in hand', patience and the anointing needed to carry out the new mission that is born when that life is born. Is it a little thing to be a missionary to just one child? Let's not deceive ourselves: *Without me, you can do nothing* – not even lead a child into the arms of God.

From this perspective, the ever-present issue of 'mixed marriage' in the church – that is, whether or not it is a sin for a believer to marry an unbeliever – would be treated differently if looked at from the angle of missions. That is to say, we would stop and ask: what impact will this marriage have on this missionary's call? What sort of 'missionary agency' will his home be? What principles is he teaching his children, when the kids work out that only one parent prays; that only one of them believes; that only one of them has pleasure in God's house, God's people, God's Word? What will these children learn when they realise that only one of their parents will be able to help with spiritual problems? That their parents have such different values, and that their yearnings, their way of diagnosing and treating the challenges of life, are so different, if not total opposites?

Thinking about things in this way means that we must go beyond the issue of the union of a Christian with a non-Christian. We might imagine two young Christians, members of the same church, but whose perceptions of mission are incompatible. If they marry only out of love and without regard to their missionary projects, the heavy weight of their unequal yoke could injure the neck of both. It is for this reason that love must be much wider and marked by more dialogue and a greater sense of responsibility – in other words, it must be *altruistic, responsible, spiritual and true,* not only in relation to sex, but also to missions.[5]

People do think twice about marrying doctors, fire-fighters, police officers, airmen and so on – to list just some activities whose peculiarities require special adjustment on the part of the spouse. Why not use a similar logic with regard to missionaries? Yes, for those who have a call to faraway places and – now that we understand the call to Jerusalem – for those who are sent to the local area. I recall the case of a girl who dated a brilliant Presbyterian seminary student, but whose lifestyle and social aspirations had no room for the idea of becoming a pastor's wife. Asked about this, she replied: 'Don't worry, I trust myself; I'll make him give up his idea. He will be a great man.' And she ended, jokingly, 'I bet all my charm and sensuality on it.'

Without wishing to pass judgement on her frivolous juvenile thinking, I couldn't help thinking that someone in that relationship was being dishonest. Or perhaps I was not informed that they didn't really intend to get married. Could be. But there is also another hypothesis: the seminary student had lost all consciousness of the demands of his mission. Maybe it got lost on the lap and among the kisses of a Delilah. Relating this case to the subject of local church mission strategies, it would be somewhat of a waste of time to hand out rational advice about church policy when the young man's emotions have already been captured. What the church and its leadership must do is create a strong, stable culture of mission.

Still on the implications of intro-mission on the normal functioning of the church, I come to the question of the family – a subject dear to any Christian church – as the focus of the church's missionary attention. My strategic proposal involves the creation of conditions and incentives so that families receive a solid foundation of teaching. After all, the fruit of the church's missionary action is the family / church. A question for you: what is it that a successful missionary leaves behind for those to whom he was sent? Let's think, for example, of the apostle Paul and all his travels. The inevitable answer is that such a missionary will leave behind either a family or a church – and the difference between the two is only a matter of size. Their nature is the same.

The ministry of reconciliation results in families. In the language of the apostle John, it produces communities, because walking in the light produces communion; it restores relationships through the work of the Cross; it opens possibilities for forgiveness, understanding, union, love, gratitude, kindness, etc. The net result is the family of God. A careful reading of Paul's letter to the Ephesians indicates that this family is the mystery that was hidden from the ancients. But the Son came, loved and died, and ever since then this family has shone forth as the most sublime outcome of a divine project focussed on relationships. So, by influencing the lives of those to whom he is sent and offering them the Gospel way of living, the missionary whose message is reconciliation is investing in a family model of relational holiness, which in and of itself reveals the wisdom, love and salvation of God. The end-result is *that the manifold wisdom of God... is made known to the rulers and authorities in the heavenly realms* (Ephesians 3:10).

However, is it possible for a missionary to instruct those to whom he is sent *in the whole will of God* (Acts 20:27) if he himself has no personal experience of a solid family foundation? Maybe he never had one? Or perhaps it was a disaster? If the missionary has no experience of the mantle of God's grace covering parental, conjugal – and not infrequently filial – problems, what is his ministry of reconciliation going to be like?

At this point, I stress that this does not contradict what I have already said: I do not mean to disqualify single missionaries, or those whom God has rescued from chaotic personal circumstances. In fact, in presenting God's ideal, we should not disqualify other forms of service or any missionary. After all, a study of Moses' call leads to the conclusion that it is God who acts. Single people and even those who are separated from their spouses have the advantage of being able to move about freely and serve in an unconstrained way. This is the idea of the apostle Paul, who proposed voluntary celibacy as a means of dedication to God. For the same reason, it is not my intention to belittle the missionary who did not have that structured family life which would have provided him with solid experiences on which to base his ministry.

So, having cleared up possible misunderstandings, my strategic proposal for churches remains: encourage the marriage of missionaries in the terms suggested above; and, by means of counselling, do not allow 'non-missionaries' to marry missionaries, for that will be an unequal yoke for both of them. Put positively, marriage among missionaries is of strategic importance for the survival of God's call, both in the newly constituted family and in the church.

A few thoughts about officials in the local church: elders, deacons, worship leaders; those involved in Christian education or social action; those who head up the different departments working with adolescents, young people, men, women, singles and so many others. I gaze at this great army of God's servants with a mixture of admiration and mercy. Yes, with the mercy of someone who looks with the eyes of his own youth, and recalls the times when he would flee from the worship service round the campfire.

I realise that the degree to which there is a formal setting apart for ministry, an investiture, varies from church to church. Some give more attention to the missionary dimension of these positions in the local church, others not so much at all. In my experience, there is generally a public and formal ceremony of commissioning for elders and deacons. As for the other office-bearers, in most churches they are prayed over as a group during the end-of-year worship time. Some churches do not even do this; in others, the moment is impressive to the point of being ostentatious. However, once the ceremony is over, there tends to be a loss of any awareness of its symbolic meaning, the awareness of a missionary sending. Words like 'call' and 'sending' are not even used – at least, that is my limited experience.

And in many churches the consequences are all too evident: elders and deacons who see themselves as being little more than administrators of an organisation, and as far as some of them are concerned, proud to know that they are useful to a church. They bring their professional experience and skills and offer them to the church in exchange for prestige and recognition – and, in some cases, in exchange for temporal power.

In giving more space to elders and deacons, I am intentionally omitting the other categories mentioned in the text – for the reason that they tend to be swallowed up by the administrative machinery of the church. And the sense of *call, commissioning* and *sending locally* becomes a mere shadow – for lack of a missionary conscience.

May all of us, all those brave non-professional workers in the Kingdom, be given the honour, the recognition, the awareness of their personal incorporation into the missionary project of Acts 1:8. May all of us seek divine power to carry out our noble mission.

At the same time, may all of us be taught about *service* and *joy*, the incarnation at work today. May each one re-programme their heart to membership of the priestly 'Order of Foot-washing', and receive the honourable accolade of being missionaries in and to their local area, of being those who will take care of the factory.

The Skin Horse

I wish to conclude with a word of comfort and encouragement to missionaries called and sent by God to their own Jerusalem. It's possible that this text has led all of us to reflect on who we are – in our families, in our places of work or study, in our local churches. Maybe some of us have re-examined our attitudes to our local church and our service in it, and have already done some soul-searching concerning our strategy there, without anyone telling us what to do – or not to do – in order to take advantage of the ideas presented in this book.

If you have felt in your heart, both that your call has been re-ignited and that you wish to recalibrate your understanding of your ministry in your family, church or place of work, I'm sure that you're feeling that the task is more arduous than we had thought. It's even possible that some have concluded that it would be preferable to be sent to the ends of the earth – have our trans-cultural missionaries been smarter after all?

I, too, am sure that *staying* in Jerusalem is as difficult a mission as that which goes out from Jerusalem. And more, that the 'Go' is as important as the *Do not leave Jerusalem* (Acts 1:4). Just to think seriously about the amount of prayer, fasting and seeking the power of the Spirit that are required in order for each one to become the Christian servant they need to be – it's all too big for me and I'm overcome by a feeling of fear.

If our hearts are in tune, yours and mine, to the point that you share these my fears, then I invite you to share a little story which has comforted and consoled me as I mull over these great themes. It has been important to me in the difficult challenge of examining the 'Go that stays', the whole message of this book. I refer to the children's story, *The Velveteen Rabbit*, part of which is a dialogue between the Velveteen Rabbit and the Skin Horse. [6] My prayer is that you too will be comforted and consoled by it.

The Skin Horse had lived longer in the nursery than any of the others. He was so old that his brown coat was bald in patches and showed the seams underneath, and most of the hairs in his tail had been pulled out to string bead necklaces. He was wise, for he had seen a long succession of mechanical toys arrive to boast and swagger, and by-and-by break their mainsprings and pass away, and he knew that they were only toys, and would never turn into anything else. For nursery magic is very strange and wonderful, and only those playthings that are old and wise and experienced like the Skin Horse understand all about it.

'What is REAL?' asked the Rabbit one day, when they were lying side-by-side near the nursery fireplace, before Nana came to tidy the room. 'Does it mean having things that buzz inside you and a stick-out handle?'

'Real isn't how you are made,' said the Skin Horse. 'It's a thing that happens to you. When a child loves you for a long, long time, not just to play with, but REALLY loves you, then you become Real.'

'Does it hurt?' asked the Rabbit.

'Sometimes,' said the Skin Horse, for he was always truthful. 'When you are Real, you don't mind being hurt.'

'Does it happen all at once, like being wound up,' he asked, 'or bit by bit?'

'It doesn't happen all at once,' said the Skin Horse. 'You become. It takes a long time. That's why it doesn't happen often to people who break easily, or have sharp edges, or who have to be carefully kept. Generally, by the time you are Real, most of your hair has been loved off, and your eyes drop out and you get loose in the joints and very shabby. But these things don't matter at all, because once you are Real, you can't be ugly, except to people who don't understand.'

'I suppose you are real?' said the Rabbit. And then he wished he had not said it, for he thought the Skin Horse might be sensitive. But the Skin Horse only smiled.

'The Boy's Uncle made me Real,' he said. 'That was a great many years ago; but once you are Real, you can't become unreal again. It lasts for always.'

Notes

[1] The author is referring here to the most widely used Portuguese translation of the Bible.

[2] A popular brand of ice cream in Brazil, corresponding to Walls in the UK.

[3] 'Commissioning' means investing with a mission.

[4] AMORESE, *Rubem, Ponto Final — a vida cristã como ela é*. 2012, Viçosa, Editora Ultimato [pp. 103-04].

[5] I develop this definition of love in my book *Sexo e Felicidade*.

[6] *The Velveteen Rabbit* (or *How Toys Become Real*) is a British children's book written by Margery Williams (also known as Margery Williams Bianco) and illustrated by William Nicholson. It chronicles the story of a stuffed rabbit's desire to become real through the love of his owner. The book was first published in 1922 and has been republished many times since.